MUSIC MAKES MEMORIES

THE GUIDE TO CHOOSING THE PERFECT WEDDING RECEPTION MUSIC

DEBORAH ARENDS AND SUSAN TODD

www.WeddingDanceSongs.net

Table of Contents

Wedding Reception Music

Music is the spice of life. It is something that none of us can do without. Especially at a wedding, music is of the essence. At most western culture wedding receptions, you will find beautiful soulful music that conveys the emotions of the bride, groom and the entire family.

The music also sets the tone at a wedding and hence should be used most appropriately to set the right mood. Whether your reception includes a formal sit down dinner, an informal buffet with light refreshments, or a backyard barbeque, music can add life to your wedding reception.

There is a specific order that music, at any wedding reception, follows. This order can be manipulated on purpose, if the bride and groom so wish, but the general order of the music is:

- Interlude
- Grand Entrance
- Dinner Music
- First Dance
- Father Daughter Dance
- Mother Son Dance
- Other Special People Dances(e.g., for Step Parents)
- General Dancing

While every family has its own traditions and festive events that take place at the wedding reception, other typical events during the wedding reception, which might have special music can be generally listed as below:

- Anniversary Dance
- Cake Cutting
- Garter Toss

- Bouquet Toss
- Last Dance

A wedding is an extremely special occasion. It is a step that unites you with the love of your life, the person you will travel the rest of your journey with. There is no better way to express the emotions you feel at such a time than with music.

FIRST WEDDING DANCE

First dance steps you take, as a newly married couple, are the most symbolic. The dance and the music that you dance to, will reflect the commitment you have made to each other and the vows you have taken for life. This song is one song that you will remember for the rest of your life and will dance to over and over, throughout your lifetime. Every time you hear it, this song will remind you of your wedding day, your First Dance, and you both will share this private moment with a twinkle in your eyes and a smile on your lips.

Your First Dance will also have all of the married guests reminiscing about their own First Dance and the love that they feel for their partner. This dance and song will also remind them of their love for you, the newly married couple. This is your dance, your time to shine – so it is extremely important that you choose this particular song with much thought and care. So how do you choose a meaningful song?

If you and your partner already have "your song", a song you have special memories attached to or a song that holds a special place in your life, and it is appropriate for you to use it for your First Dance, you are all set. Many couples do not have a special song, or the special song that they do have might not be appropriate for a First Dance (e.g., it might be very hard to dance to, or may have inappropriate lyrics). In such a case, new options will need to be explored.

There are thousands of possibilities for a First Dance – but the difficult part is to narrow down the choices and choose the best one for you, as a couple. This is where our special book for wedding reception music can help you out. We have compiled an extensive list of meaningful, danceable songs from a variety of music genres and provided comments about each of those songs. You can search alphabetically by song title, or by type of dance. If you are connected to the Internet, you can also listen to a snippet of each song and/or read the song lyrics.

Choosing Your First Wedding Dance Song

While making a decision about your first wedding dance song, from a gamut of options available, there are certain factors that you need to consider. These things, if kept in mind, can easily help you pick out the best song for your First Dance.

Factors that matter most when choosing a song include the lyrics of the song (is it meaningful to you) and the speed and dance style of the song (is it danceable for you).

IS THE SONG MEANINGFUL?

To make sure the song is meaningful to you, be certain to read the lyrics of the song and consider whether the lyrics express your relationship, your mood and your emotions most appropriately.

Ideally, the song lyrics will express the love you and your partner feel toward each other or will otherwise express an important aspect of your relationship. It might represent the exact moment when you just knew that "this is the one." The song might be a musical snapshot of the time, place, or circumstances of when or how you knew you had fallen deeply in love and wanted to spend the rest of your lives together. It could also reflect the expectations you have regarding your future together or how you see your married life unfold with each other.

When you hear the song, it must automatically remind you of your desire to spend the rest of your lives together or of the wishes you have for your partner and your relationship. Usually, when you hear the song that is 'meant for you', you just know it!

It is important to note if whether there are things about the songs that make them inappropriate, such as veiled sexual innuendos you'd rather not have, or whether the song was actually written for another reason that might not be appropriate. Some songs have titles that sound appropriate, but are actually about heartbreak, adultery, or other themes that you may prefer to avoid at your wedding. Wikipedia is another useful resource that provides information about many of the songs you might want to consider.

It is also a good idea to listen to at least a short snippet of each song that you are considering, in order to ascertain if it has the right sound for you.

IS THE SONG DANCEABLE?

Simply choosing the song on the basis of lyrics and 'feel' will not do the job. You will also need to make sure that it is actually danceable. To make certain that the song is danceable, one of the first things you need to consider is whether you want to do a specific dance[1] (such as waltz, foxtrot, rumba, etc.) or to sway back and forth without doing anything specific.

It is important that you realize that your First Dance is not just a dance, it is a performance! The two of you are dancing in the spotlight, (metaphorically, or even literally depending on your venue) in front of an audience (you wedding guests, who fortunately will be supportive and compassionate no matter what you do).

Because there will likely be many pictures taken and very possibly a video too, we highly recommend that you choose a specific dance type and learn a few basic steps, along with the proper dance frame, and take time to practice to your dance. You will likely feel more confident and relaxed, once you have rehearsed, and your dance will be more visually appealing to your audience as well as on your wedding reception video. Keeping this in mind, we have categorized the First Dance song recommendations by type of dance.

If you are going to simply sway back and forth, then how danceable the song is does not necessarily need to be a consideration, although dancing on the beat is still generally preferable. If a song has a long introduction that has a hard-to-hear beat, then it may not be a song you want to choose (unless you, or someone on your behalf, remove the introduction with music editing software).

If, however, you DO decide to do a specific dance type, how danceable the song is, most certainly, is an important criterion while selecting the song. To be considered danceable, a song should have a beat that you can hear throughout the song. The song should also have an appropriate speed – not too fast and

---

[1]For a description of the different dances, see the very end of this report.

definitely not too slow. Songs that are too slow are actually very hard to dance to, in general, and songs that are too fast will not allow you to do the dance steps as easily and precisely.

The tables in the "Longer List" below indicate how fast each song is (in both measures per minute, for those of you who know a lot about specific dance styles, and also categorized as Slow, Ideal, and Fast).

OTHER CONSIDERATIONS

Do you want your song to date your wedding? If your answer to this question is a yes, you might first want to decide on the year of your choice, if whether you want a period wedding or a modern one. If you want something modern, new, or hip that sends a message that you were married in the modern era, then by all means, you should choose a contemporary song. However, if you don't want to date your wedding, you may want to go with a classic. There is a reason they have stood the test of time and are called classics.

How long should your dance be? This is another important consideration while choosing the best song. Less is more in this case. It is better if your guests wish for more, rather than get bored and lose interest. A five minute dance is too long if you want your guests to stay interested and pay attention to your entire dance. A good target is around 2-3 minutes. That might not sound like much time, but when you are the only couple on the dance floor with everyone watching, it can seem like an eternity!

If you choose a song that is longer than 2-3 minutes, you can ask your DJ to fade it out after 2-3 minutes, or you (or someone on your behalf) can shorten the song to an appropriate length. If you shorten a song, it is advisable that you listen to the whole song and choose the verses that are most meaningful to you. Also, you must determine if there are parts of the song that you want to exclude (verses you don't like as much, or a long introduction that has no discernible beat, for example).

In the "Longer List" below, the length of each song is provided so you will know if whether it needs to be shortened or faded.

FATHER-DAUGHTER AND MOTHER-SON DANCE SONGS

Father-Daughter Dance and Mother-Son Dances are beautiful ways to acknowledge the special relationship between you and your parent, and to honor your love and respect for each other. Thus picking the right song, one that reflects your special relationship, is important.

As a daughter or son gets married, the parents, in a sense, let go of them, and watch another person become the focus of their child's world. This can be an extremely emotional moment. Your relationship will be changed forever, and your special dance is a wonderful way to mark this transition.

During the dance itself, you can share the moment quietly or talk of many things – the happy memories from your past, your hopes and goals for the future, or whatever emotions you go through at that special moment. That really doesn't matter, but what does matter is that you are sharing a precious moment together that each of you will remember forever.

Choosing the Songs

Most of the advice for choosing a First Dance song can also be applied to the Father-Daughter and Mother-Son Song. There are a few differences though, because it is not a romantic couple who is doing the dancing.

Your father and mother's opinion of the song matters! In fact, it is possible that he or she already has a song in mind. But if not, consider selecting a few possibilities that you like and sharing them with each other. This can also be taken as a chance to connect with your parent and create a special memory together.

To make sure the song is meaningful; you must read the lyrics of the song and consider whether the lyrics express your relationship. There are a number of songs that have been written specifically for Father-Daughter or Mother-Son dances, although many other songs are appropriate as well.

RECEPTION MUSIC SUGGESTIONS

INTERLUDE

The guests typically arrive at the reception before the wedding party and the bride and groom. Often the bride and groom have their pictures taken while the guests make their way to the reception. Gentle, soft background music usually accompanies this period of time, while cocktails and hors d'oeuvres are typically served, called the Interlude. This music will be the first that your guests hear and will go a long way in setting the tone and mood of the wedding.

We recommend that you have your DJ or band choose the Interlude music as per the theme of your wedding. If you are planning to have an "iPod Wedding", we suggest classical music, harp music, New Age music, or any other music without words or lyrics. Some choices include:

- **Romantic Wedding Music on the Harp** (tracks 4-17; **tracks 1-3 would be best in the wedding ceremony rather** than the reception)
- **Wedding Reception - Best Instrumental Songs**
- **Beautiful Wedding - Classical Music for the Wedding Dinner**
- **Beautiful Wedding - Jazz for the Wedding Dinner**
- **Dinner For Two - Ultimate Classical Piano Background Music for Dinner**
- **Ultimate Wedding Collection: Dinner Music**

Grand Entrance

The Grand Entrance is when the Bride and Groom arrive at the reception with much fanfare. Often the wedding party is announced first, as they enter the room. The Bride and Groom come in last and are introduced as the newly married couple. This is a special moment as your guests are in a festive mood, after the wedding ceremony, and wish to celebrate YOU, as a couple.

You could have your DJ or band select special music for the Grand Entrance, or you could choose a dramatic or celebratory song such as:

- **A Fifth of Beethoven** (a hip, disco-like version of Beethoven's Fifth Symphony) by Walter Murphy
- **Also sprach Zarathustra** (from "2001: A Space Odessy" by Berliner Philharmoniker)
- **Another One Bites the Dust** by Queen
- **Celebration** by Kool & The Gang
- **Get the Party Started** by P!nk
- **Here Comes The Broad** (An Adaptation Of Wagner's "Lohengrin" And Mendelssohn's "A Midsummer Night's Dream") by Brian Setzer
- **I Gotta Feeling** by The Black Eyed Peas

Dinner Music

During dinner, soft background music is once again played, suitable to your wedding style. There is a lot of socializing during this period and generally people want to share the excitement and talk. At this time, it is important to make sure that the conversation is not drowned out by the music.

We recommend that you have your DJ or band choose the dinner music. If you are having an "iPod Wedding", we suggest you go for the same type of music as the one playing during the Interlude.

First Dance

The dancing doesn't begin until the First Dance of the Bride and Groom. This is a very special moment when you take the floor for the first time as a married couple. The choice of song is important for this dance. It should convey the meaning of your relationship and love for each other. It should also be appropriate for the type of dance you want to do.

We HIGHLY recommend that you choose this song carefully. The various factors that you must consider while choosing the song for this dance have already been discussed in a previous chapter of this book. Below is a short list of recommended First Dance songs, specific to different dance styles, provided for your consideration.

Short List[2]:

- Foxtrot
  - **I Love You** by Frank Sinatra

---

[2]The "Short Lists" are our top choices for special dance songs for each of the most common dance styles for a First Dance, Father-Daughter Dance and Mother-Son Dance. These songs are beautiful songs in their own right, they have great lyrics for the particular dance, they are a good tempo (speed) for dancing, and they have a clear beat and rhythm to help you keep your dance on track. Some of them are a little on the long side (more than 3 minutes), so you might consider having your DJ fade the song out if you are using a recording. Each of the songs in the Short List is also in the following "Long List" section below, where more information, such as comments,is provided about each song.

- "I love you. I love you. Is all that I can say..."
- **It Had to Be You** by Harry Connick, Jr.
  - "It had to be you, it had to be you, I wandered around, and finally found..."
- **Orange Colored Sky** by Natalie Cole
  - "I was walking along, minding my business, when out of an orange-colored sky..."
- **The Way You Look Tonight** by Frank Sinatra
  - "Someday, when I'm awfully low, when the world is cold..."
- **You're My Best Friend** by Queen
  - "Ooo, you make me live, whatever this world can give to me, it's you, you're all I see..."

- Nightclub Two Step
  - **(Everything I Do) I Do It For You** by Bryan Adams (can also be danced as a Slow Dance)
    - "Look into my eyes – you will see what you mean to me..."
  - **Here And Now** by Luther Vandross
    - "One look in your eyes and there I see, just what you mean to me..."
  - **I Knew I Loved You** by Savage Garden
    - "Maybe it's intuition, but some things you just don't question..."
  - **Love Never Fails** by Jim Brickman
    - "Love, love is patient, love is kind, love does not worry, does not boast..."
  - **This I Promise You** by N Sync
    - "When the visions around you, bring tears to your eyes, and all that surround you, are secrets and lies..."
  - **You're The Inspiration** by Chicago
    - "You know our love was meant to be, the kind of love that lasts forever..."

- Rumba
  - **Can You Feel The Love Tonight** by Elton John

- "There's a calm surrender to the rush of day when the heat of a rolling wind can be turned away…"
  - **Here We Stand** by Anthony Carter
    - "Here we are, face to face, brought here together, by God's amazing grace…"
  - **Love of a Lifetime** by Firehouse
    - "I guess the time was right for us to say, we'd take our time and live our lives together day by day…"
  - **The Way You Look Tonight** by Michael Bublé
    - "Someday, when I'm awfully low, when the world is cold…"
  - **You Are The Sunshine Of My Life** by Stevie Wonder
    - "You are the sunshine of my life, that's why I'll always be around…"
  - **You're Still The One** by Shania Twain
    - "Looks like we made it. Look how far we've come my baby. We mighta took the long way…"
  - **Wedding Song [There Is Love]** by Noel Paul Stookey
    - "He is now to be among you at the calling of your hearts. Rest assured this troubadour is acting on His part. The union of your spirits here has caused Him to remain…"

- Slow Dance
  - **(Everything I Do) I Do It For You** by Bryan Adams (can also be danced as a Nightclub Two Step)
    - "Look into my eyes – you will see what you mean to me…"
  - **Dance with Me** by Anthony Carter
    - "The day is here, and the time has come, for you and I together as one…"
  - **Endless Love** by Diana Ross and Lionel Richie
    - "My love, there's only you in my life, the only thing that's right…"

- ○ **Making Memories of Us** by Keith Urban
  - ▪ "I'm gonna be here for you baby, and I'll be a man of my word..."

- • Waltz
  - ○ **Between Now and Forever** by Bryan White
    - ▪ "I can't believe that I've found you, fate did a number on me..."
  - ○ **Could I Have This Dance** by Anne Murray
    - ▪ "I'll always remember the song they were playing, the first time we danced and I knew..."
  - ○ **Give Me Forever (I Do)** by John Tesh
    - ▪ "Looking out, I see and I know just how much you're a part of me..."
  - ○ **I Will Always Return** by Bryan Adams (track 15)
    - ▪ "I hear the wind call my name, the sound that leads me home again..."
  - ○ **You Light Up My Life** by Whitney Houston
    - ▪ "So many nights I sit by my window, waiting for someone to sing me his song..."

Father Daughter Dance

The next dance is typically the Father Daughter dance. This is where the bride's father takes the floor with his daughter. You may have a special song that the two of you love or a song that characterizes your relationship. Your father may have a special song in mind, so make sure to ask him before starting your search.

While the Father Daughter songs are special, it is important to remember that they will be different from the First Dance songs because they will not be romantic like them. The factors you must consider have been discussed in a previous chapter of this book. Below is a short list of songs, most appropriate, as per dance styles, for your consideration.

Short List:

- Foxtrot
  - **Ain't that Love** by Ray Charles
    - "Now, baby when you sigh (when you sigh) I wanna sigh with you..."
  - **Thank Heaven for Little Girls** by Merle Haggard
    - "Thank heaven for little girls, for little girls get bigger every day..."
  - **The Way You Look Tonight** by Frank Sinatra
    - "Someday, when I'm awfully low, when the world is cold..."
  - **Too Marvelous For Words** by Frank Sinatra
    - "You're just too marvelous, too marvelous for words, like "glorious", "glamorous" and that old standby "amorous"..."

- Nightclub Two Step
  - **Daddy's Angel** by Anthony Carter
    - "I'm giving you away, but I'm not letting go, the memories, they flood my mind of the little girl I know..."
  - **My Little Girl (from My Friend Flicka)** by Tim McGraw
    - "Gotta hold on easy as I let you go, gonna tell you how much I love you, though you think you already know..."
  - **Over the Rainbow** by Israel "IZ" Kamakawiwo'ole
    - "Somewhere over the rainbow way up high, and the dreams that you dream of once in a lullaby..."
  - **Times of Your Life** by Paul Anka
    - "Good morning, yesterday, you wake up and time has slipped away..."
  - **What A Wonderful World** by Louis Armstrong

- "I see trees of green, red roses too, I see them bloom for me and you..."
- Rumba
  - **A Song For My Daughter** by Mikki Viereck OR Ray Allaire
    - "Just once upon a yesterday I held you in my arms; you grew into a little girl with lovely childhood charms..."
  - **Because You Loved Me** by Celine Dion
    - "For all those times you stood by me for all the truth that you made me see..."
  - **Can You Feel the Love Tonight** by Elton John
    - "There's a calm surrender to the rush of day when the heat of a rolling wind can be turned away..."
  - **Isn't She Lovely** by Stevie Wonder
    - "Isn't she lovely, isn't she wonderful, isn't she precious, less than one minute old..."
  - **There You'll Be** by Faith Hill
    - "When I think back on these times and the dreams we left behind, I'll be glad 'cause I was blessed to get to have you in my life..."
  - **Wind Beneath My Wings** by Bette Midler
    - "It must have been cold there in my shadow, to never have sunlight on your face..."

- Slow Dance
  - **Blessed** by Elton John
    - "Hey you, you're a child in my head - you haven't walked yet, your first words have yet to be said - but I swear you'll be blessed...
  - **Here for You** by Neil Young
    - "When your summer days come tumbling down and you find yourself alone..."
  - **Unforgettable** by Natalie Cole and Nat King Cole
    - "Unforgettable, that's what you are. Unforgettable, though near or far..."

- Two Step[3] or (fast) Foxtrot
  - **Daddy's Hands** by Holly Dunn
    - "I remember Daddy's hands folded silently in prayer, and reaching out to hold me when I had a nightmare..."

- Waltz
  - **Daddy's Little Girl** by Al Martino
    - "You're Daddy's Little Girl, you're the end of the rainbow - my Pot of Gold..."
  - **Sunrise, Sunset** by Complete Wedding Music Resource
    - "Is this the little girl I carried? Is this the little boy at play? I don't remember growing older When did they...?"
  - **The Lover's Waltz** by Jay Ungar and Molly Mason
    - Instrumental (no lyrics)
  - **Turn Around** by Perry Como
    - "Turnaround, turnaround, turnaround and you're a young girl going out of the door..."
  - **What The World Needs Now Is Love** by Jackie Deshannon
    - "What the world needs now, is love, sweet love, it's the only thing that there's just too little of..."

Mother Son Dance

Following the Father Daughter dance is optionally the Mother Son dance. The Mother Son dance is another very special dance where the mother of the groom dances with her son. Sometimes the Father Daughter and Mother Son dances are combined, in which case you will not need to select a separate song for this

---

[3]Note that Two Step (a country dance) and Nightclub Two Step (a "love song" dance) are completely different dances.

dance. However, if you do have a separate Mother-Son dance lined up, then you will have to be very thoughtful while selecting a song for this special dance. The mother may also have a special song picked out that she's been thinking about for a long time, so make sure to ask her! These songs are not supposed to be as romantic as the First Dance song.

Following is a short list of songs that are appropriate for Mother-Son dances. You may go through the list and make a selection, according to the dance style you have chosen.

Short List:

- Foxtrot
  - **Ain't that Love** by Ray Charles
    - "Now, baby when you sigh (when you sigh) I wanna sigh with you…"
  - **The Way You Look Tonight** by Frank Sinatra
    - "Someday, when I'm awfully low, when the world is cold…"
  - **Too Marvelous For Words** by Frank Sinatra
    - "You're just too marvelous, too marvelous for words, like "glorious", "glamorous" and that old standby "amorous"…"

- Nightclub Two Step
  - **Over the Rainbow** by Israel "IZ" Kamakawiwo'ole
    - "Somewhere over the rainbow way up high, and the dreams that you dream of once in a lullaby…"
  - **A Song for Mama** by Boyz II Men
    - "You taught me everything, and everything you've given me - I always keep it inside…"
  - **Times of Your Life** by Paul Anka
    - "Good morning, yesterday, you wake up and time has slipped away…"

- Rumba

- o **A Mother's Song** by Anthony Carter
  - "Tying little shoe laces, wiping off dirty faces are just a couple of things that a mother will do"
- o **Because You Loved Me** by Celine Dion
  - "For all those times you stood by me for all the truth that you made me see…"
- o **Can You Feel the Love Tonight** by Elton John
  - "There's a calm surrender to the rush of day when the heat of a rolling wind can be turned away…"
- o **The Way You Look Tonight** by Michael Bublé
  - "Someday, when I'm awfully low, when the world is cold…"
- o **There You'll Be** by Faith Hill
  - "When I think back on these times and the dreams we left behind, I'll be glad 'cause I was blessed to get to have you in my life…"
- o **Wind Beneath My Wings** by Bette Midler
  - "It must have been cold there in my shadow, to never have sunlight on your face…"

- Slow Dance
  - o **Blessed** by Elton John
    - "Hey you, you're a child in my head - you haven't walked yet, your first words have yet to be said - but I swear you'll be blessed…
  - o **Here for You** by Neil Young
    - "When your summer days come tumbling down and you find yourself alone…"
  - o **Memories** by Elvis Presley
    - "Memories, pressed between the pages of my mind; memories, sweetened through the ages just like wine…"
  - o **Unforgettable** by Natalie Cole and Nat King Cole
    - "Unforgettable, that's what you are. Unforgettable, though near or far…"

- Waltz

- o **A Song for My Son** by Donna Lee Honeywell
  - ▪ "I don't know where the time has gone since those little boy days..."
- o **Mama** by B.J. Thomas
  - ▪ "Who's the one who tied your shoe when you were young and knew just when to come and see what you had done...?"
- o **Sunrise, Sunset** by Complete Wedding Music Resource
  - ▪ "Is this the little girl I carried? Is this the little boy at play? I don't remember growing older When did they...?"
- o **The Lover's Waltz** by Jay Ungar and Molly Mason
  - ▪ Instrumental (no lyrics)

Other Special People (step parents, for example) Dances

You may have other very special people in your life that you want to honor with a special dance such as best friends, siblings, uncles or aunts and step parents. Many of the songs that are appropriate for the Father-Daughter Dance and Mother-Son Dance are appropriate for these dances as well.

Anniversary Dance

The Anniversary Dance is not as traditional as the three dances above. However, if there are many generations of people at your wedding, you may consider having this dance. This dance begins with all married couples on the floor. Subsequently, couples must leave the floor as they are called. The couple that has spent the maximum number of years being married together is the last on the floor.

Generally, the DJ or band leader will announce that all couples married less than a day must leave the floor first. Then, less than 1 year, less than 5 years, 10 years, 15 years, 20 years, 30 years, so on and so forth, must leave the floor. Knowing your guests, you can come up with good cut off points for leaving the floor. Finally, you want to make sure all guests have left the floor except for the longest married couple.

It is a nice touch to play the song that that couple had danced to, years before, for their First Dance, as the last song in the series. Since many songs are usually played in succession for this dance, you may want to cue up songs that different people from your wedding danced to as a special touch. Otherwise, general love songs are appropriate. Ask your DJ or band to choose the songs, or consider the following:

- **Romantic Mood Love Songs**
- **The Love Album**
- **10 Great Christian Love Songs : Vol.1**
- **Love Songs We Used to Share**
- **Love Songs: 14 All-time Favorites**

General Dancing

After the family dances are over, there is typically general dancing for the guests. A mix of faster upbeat songs and slower more romantic songs are most appropriate.

If you have a DJ or a band, having them choose the music for this portion will take the pressure off of you. They typically have a large repertoire, from which to choose. They can cue up some of the most popular songs for you and your guests. If you are having an "iPod Wedding", a good choice is to buy compilations of love songs (see list above for Anniversary Dance) and party music, such as:

- **NOW That's What I Call Party Hits**
- **NOW That's What I Call Club Hits**
- **50s Jukebox Hits**
- **The '60s Hits**
- **Pure 70's**
- **'80s Party**
- **80s & '90s Dance Hits (Re-Recorded / Remastered Versions)**

Throughout the evening, general dancing will typically be punctuated with other special events, such as cake cutting, and the garter and bouquet toss.

Cake Cutting Song

The wedding cake cutting is another very special event, which the bride and groom partake in. The wedding cake has a long history, dating back to the Roman Empire. Many traditions, in connection with the wedding cake, have come and gone over the years. In the early days, grooms would eat part of a special loaf of barley bread, baked for the wedding, and then break the rest of it over the bride's head. History suggests this symbolized breaking the bride's virginal state and the groom's subsequent dominance over her. Guests would scramble to get pieces of the crumbs to take home for good luck and fertility. Thankfully, this chauvinistic tradition did not survive over the years.

In Medieval England, guests would stack little cakes in a large pile, and the bride and groom would try to kiss over the pile. If successful, it was a sign of their future fertility. A modern version of the wedding cake is to stack donuts or have a tiered display of cupcakes or other sweets, harkening back to the medieval pile of little cakes. Who knew?

Traditionally, it was the bride's duty to cut the cake and serve it to the wedding guests. As the number of guests grew larger, the cakes did too, and they also became multi-tiered over time. Initially the icing was made very thick and hard to support the tiers, and assistance was required to cut the cake. Thus cake cutting became a joint effort between the bride and groom.

Part of the cake cutting tradition, that has survived, is for the bride and groom to feed each other from the first slice, demonstrating their mutual commitment to provide for one another. Naturally, feeding each other is sometimes accidentally, or purposefully, messy. It can be a tender or silly moment, depending on the couple.

Nowadays, couples frequently have music playing during the cake cutting that has to do with food or hunger, or in some way says something about the nature of their relationship. Some songs to consider for cutting the cake are:

- **Cut The Cake** by Average White Band
- **Eat It** by Weird Al Yankovic
- **Grow Old With You** (from The Wedding Singer) by Stephen Lynch
- **Happy Together** by The Nylons
- **How Sweet It Is** by James Taylor
- **Hungry Eyes** by Eric Carmen
- **I Got You Babe** by Sonny & Cher
- **Ice Cream** by Sarah McLachlan
- **It's Your Love** by Tim McGraw & Faith Hill
- **Jaws Theme** by John Williams
- **Love Me Tender** by Elvis Presley
- **Mack the Knife** by Michael Bublé
- **Oh Yeah** by Yello
- **Peter Gunn** Theme by Henry Mancini

- **Recipe for Love** by Harry Connick, Jr.
- **Sugar, Sugar** by The Archies
- **Sweet Dreams (Are Made Of This)** by Eurythmics
- **Sweets For My Sweet** by The Drifters
- **That's Amore** by Dean Martin
- **Yummy, Yummy, Yummy** by Ohio Express

Two other songs that are frequently recommended for the Cake Cutting are:

- **The First Cut Is The Deepest** by Cat Stevens
- **Cuts Like a Knife** by Bryan Adams

However, these last two songs are actually about being unlucky at love. Be sure to check out the lyrics if you use this song, or have a very short section of the song prepared that uses just the part of the song you want to hear while cutting the cake.

Garter Toss Song

Garter tossing is a very interesting and fun event at a wedding reception. The bride and groom partake in this traditional event with much ado and laughter. There might be variations in how the garter is obtained, depending upon different family traditions.

There are several interesting theories about how the garter toss tradition came into existence. Apparently in 14th century France, it was considered lucky to get a fragment of the bride's clothing. They would grab at her dress and literally tear pieces off. Not liking this, brides began throwing personal articles, such as the garter, stocking, bouquet, etc., to the guests to appease them. Later, it became the best man's job to obtain the garter and distribute pieces of it to the guests. Again not liking to be manhandled, brides allowed one garter to dangle loosely, making it easy to reach and remove.

Another theory suggests, the garter tradition was related to consummating the marriage. In medieval times, guests would accompany the newlyweds to the bridal chamber to witness the consummation. The garter was taken as proof. Apparently, this was sometimes pretty rowdy and people sometimes got injured, so to avoid this situation, the groom would toss the bride's garter to the men to distract them as he whisked his new bride away. Over time, the tradition changed, but the garter was (and is) still a lucky prize.

Nowadays, the groom will often make a big show of removing the garter before tossing it to the single men, thus a raunchy song is often selected for the garter removal and toss. Often, the man who catches the garter will dance with the woman who catches the bouquet, kicking off the next round of dancing.

Popular songs for the garter toss include:

- **Another One Bites the Dust** by Queen
- **Bad Boy For Life** by P. Diddy
- **Bad Boys (Theme From Cops)** by Inner Circle
- **Bad to the Bone** by George Thorogood & The Destroyers
- **Cherry Pie** by Warrant
- **Da Ya Think I'm Sexy?** by Rod Stewart
- **Do You Wanna Touch Me** by Joan Jett
- **Fever** by Elvis Presley
- **Foxey Lady** by Jimi Hendrix
- **Girls, Girls, Girls** by Motley Crue
- **Hot In Herre** by Nelly
- **Hot Legs** by Rod Stewart
- **(I Wanna Be) Your Underwear** by Bryan Adams
- **I Want Candy** by Bow Wow Wow
- **I'm Too Sexy** by Right Said Fred
- **Keep Your Hands To Yourself** by The Georgia Satellites

- **Killer Queen** by Queen
- **Kiss** by Prince
- **Lay Your Hands On Me** by Bon Jovi
- **Legs** by ZZ Top
- **Let's Get It On** by Marvin Gaye
- **Oh Yeah** by Yello
- **Peter Gunn Theme** by Henry Mancini
- **Push It** by Salt N' Pepa
- **Sexbomb** by Tom Jones
- **Sexual Healing** by Marvin Gaye
- **SexyBack** by Justin Timberlake
- **The Stripper** by David Rose
- **Theme From Mission Impossible**
- **Thong Song** by Sisqo
- **Wild Thing** by Tone Loc
- **Wild Thing** by The Troggs
- **You Can Leave Your Hat On** by Joe Cocker
- **You Sexy Thing** by Hot Chocolate

Bouquet Toss Song

Bouquet tossing is a fun-filled event where all the single ladies line up to catch the bouquet, tossed by the bride. As noted in the garter section above, the bouquet toss likely started as a way to keep the bride's clothing intact from the hordes of guests who wanted a piece of luck. This has evolved into the tradition of tossing a bouquet (nowadays often a special "toss bouquet" and not the bride's real bouquet) to the single women, and the lucky one who catches the bouquet is said to be the next to marry.

Although bouquet tossing, sometimes, may lead to injury as the women trip over each other trying to catch the bouquet (doh!), this fun tradition has lived on. Some good songs to consider include:

- **Dirrty** by Christina Aguilera
- **Diamonds are a Girl's Best Friend** by Marilyn Monroe
- **Girls Night Out** by The Judds
- **Girls, Girls, Girls** by Motley Crue
- **Girls Just Want To Have Fun** by Cyndi Lauper
- **Hot Girls in Love** by Loverboy
- **I Wanna Have Some Fun** by Samantha Fox
- **I Want Candy** by Bow Wow Wow
- **It's Raining Men** by The Weather Girls
- **Just A Girl** by No Doubt
- **Ladies Night** by Kool & the Gang
- **Lady Marmalade** by Christina Aguilara, Lil' Kim, Mya & P!nk
- **Let's Get Loud** by Jenifer Lopez
- **Like A Virgin** by Madonna
- **Man! I Feel Like A Woman!** by Shania Twain
- **Milkshake** by Kelis
- **Oh Yeah** by Yello
- **Super Freak** by Rick James
- **That Girl** by Maxi Priest
- **Theme From Mission Impossible**
- **This One's For The Girls** by Martina McBride
- **Whatever Lola Wants** by Sarah Vaughn
- **Where My Girls At** by 702
- **Whipped Cream** (Dating Game Theme) by Herb Alpert
- **Wild Thing** by Tone Loc
- **Wild Thing** by The Troggs
- **You Can't Take The Honky Tonk Out Of The Girl** by Brooks & Dunn

Alternatively, some brides have "break apart" bouquets created, which separate into many little bouquets, which they then distribute to various guests (e.g., bride's mother, groom's

32

mother, bridesmaids, single women – whomever the bride wants to honor). If you do something like this, choose a song that represents the mood you want to create, which could be from the bouquet toss list above, or a love song from an album mentioned in this report, or a song about friendship, such as:

- **Anytime You Need A Friend** by Mariah Carey
- **Celebration** by Kool & The Gang
- **Everybody Have Fun Tonight** by Wang Chung
- **Friends** by Elton John
- **Heroes and Friends** by Randy Travis
- **Kind and Generous** by Natalie Merchant
- **Lean on Me** by Bill Withers
- **Shower the People** by James Taylor
- **Thank You** by Dido
- **That's What Friends Are For** by Dionne Warrick & Friends
- **There You'll Be** by Faith Hill
- **We Are Family** by Sister Sledge
- **What About Your Friends** by TLC
- **Wind Beneath My Wings** by Bette Midler
- **You've Got a Friend** by James Taylor
- **You've Got a Friend in Me (from Toy Story)** by Randy Newman & Lyle Lovett

Last Dance

The Last Dance wraps up the formal celebration. After the Last Dance, the bride and groom leave the reception. The reception may continue on, or it might be over - the choice might depend on the venue and your DJ/band. If you want everyone to leave after the Last Dance, a good choice is for the song itself to convey a farewell theme.

Couples usually go one of several ways with the Last Dance song. One choice is play an "End of Evening" song that lets guests know the party is over and it's time to go. Another choice is to play a nice romantic slow song that everyone, including the bride and groom, can dance to. If you have trouble deciding between two songs for your first dance, you could use one of the songs as the Last Dance. Another choice is to play an upbeat celebration song so everyone leaves on a high note. The choice is up to you!

End of Evening Last Dance Songs
- **Closing Time** by Semisonic
  - "Closing time - time for you to go out, go out into the world..."
- **Goodnight Sweetheart Goodnight** by Spaniels
  - "Goodnight, sweetheart, well, it's time to go, ..."
- **Happy Trails** by Van Halen
  - "Happy trails to you, until we meet again..."
- **Last Dance** by Donna Summer
  - "Last dance, last dance for love, yes, it's my last chance for romance tonight..."
- **Last Dance** by Frank Sinatra
  - "It's the last dance, we've come to the last dance, they're dimming the lights down, they're hoping we'll go..."
- **The Party's Over** by Nat King Cole
  - "The party's over, it's time to call it a day..."

Romantic Last Dance Songs
- **Always And Forever** by Heatwave
  - "Always and forever, each moment with you, is just like a dream to me that somehow came true..."
- **Could I Have This Dance** by Anne Murray
  - "I'll always remember the song they were playin', the first time we danced and I knew, ..."
- **From This Moment On** by Shania Twain
  - "I do swear that I'll always be there. I'd give anything and everything and I will always care..."

- **Lady in Red** by Chris Deburgh
  - "I've never seen you looking so lovely as you did tonight, I've never seen you shine so bright..."
- **Save The Best For Last** by Vanessa Williams
  - "Sometimes the snow comes down in June, sometimes the sun goes 'round the moon..."
- **Truly, Madly, Deeply** by Savage Garden
  - "I'll be your dream, I'll be your wish, I'll be your fantasy..."
- **Unforgettable** by Natalie Cole and Nat King Cole
  - "Unforgettable, that's what you are. Unforgettable, though near or far..."
- **What a Wonderful World** by Louis Armstrong
  - "I see trees of green, red roses too, I see them bloom for me and you..."
- **Wonderful Tonight** by Eric Clapton
  - "It's late in the evening; she's wondering what clothes to wear. She puts on her make-up and brushes her long blonde hair..."
- **You're Still The One** by Shania Twain
  - "When I first saw you, I saw love. And the first time you touched me, I felt love..."

Upbeat Last Dance Songs
- **Good Riddance (Time Of Your Life)** by Green Day
  - "Another turning point, a fork stuck in the road, time grabs you by the wrist, directs you where to go..."
- **How Your Love Makes Me Feel** by Diamond Rio
  - "I'm no poet and I know it, I don't use five dollar words..."
- **I've Had The Time Of My Life** by Bill Medley & Jennifer Warnes
  - "Now I've had the time of my life, No I never felt like this before..."
- **Kiss Him Goodbye** by The Nylons
  - "Na na na na, na na na na, hey hey-ey, goodbye..."
- **Love Will Keep Us Together** by Captain and Tennille

- o "Love, love will keep us together, think of me babe whenever…"
- **New York, New York** by Frank Sinatra
  - o "Start spreading the news, I'm leaving today. I want to be a part of it - New York, New York…"
- **Save the Last Dance For Me** by Michael Bublé
  - o "You can dance-every dance with the guy who gives you the eye, let him hold you tight…"

Upbeat (Breakup) Last Dance Song
- **Hit the Road Jack** by Ray Charles
  - o "Hit the road Jack and don't you come back no more, no more, no more, no more…"

First Dance, Father-Daughter Dance, and Mother-Son Dance Long Lists

The Long Lists

The following tables provide lots of great, meaningful, danceable songs for special wedding dances. Some were written specifically for the First Dance, the Father-Daughter Dance or the Mother-Son Dance, and some are more general love songs. Some have highly romantic lyrics, some are whimsical, and some have no lyrics at all. Our long lists of songs have a huge variety of songs to choose from, according to the dance style you wish to choose for each event.

Although it is nice to honor the father of the bride and the mother of the groom with separate dances, you can combine the Father Daughter and Mother Son dances. Make sure you choose a song that is appropriate for both if you go with this decision.

We have read the lyrics of every song to make sure they are meaningful and appropriate for the special wedding dances, and we strongly encourage you to read the lyrics too. In a few cases, we have included some commonly recommended songs that have, what we consider to be, somewhat questionable lyrics, and the comment for such songs indicates this. Just because we think a song has questionable (or great) lyrics doesn't mean you will agree, which is why we recommend that you read the complete lyrics yourself for the songs that you are considering. You can find all of the lyrics to every song on our website: http://WeddingDanceSongs.net.

The comment section also indicates a few songs that are a bit harder to dance to and that you might want to avoid if you are a beginner dancer.

The tables below indicate the speed of each song in two ways: speed category (Slow, Ideal, Fast) and measures per minute[4] (MPM). Speed category is relative to the type of dance and is based on MPM. For beginners, speed category is really all that matters. Songs marked as Ideal are typically the easiest to dance to, whereas songs marked as slow tend to be the most difficult to dance to (except for Viennese/Hesitation waltz, which is most difficult if faster than ideal). Because there are individual differences (e.g., a physical condition that makes moving slowly more comfortable, or nervous excitement that makes moving faster easier), you should take your specific situation into account when using the speed category to help make your decision. If you have software to do it, you can also consider speeding up or slowing down a song that you like, if its tempo is not ideal.

The first table provides an extensive list of popular, meaningful, danceable First Dance songs, sorted alphabetically by song title. You might find that looking through a list of lots of songs is a great way to get the creative juices flowing. It may make you think about songs you might not have considered otherwise. The tables include the dance type for each song, as well.

The second table provides an extensive list for Father-Daughter and Mother-Son Dance songs.

---

[4]Dancers have historically categorized music by the number of measures of music that fit in one minute (whereas musicians typically count beats per minute, or BPM). Waltz has 3 beats per measure, thus a waltz with 30 MPM = 90 beats BPM. The other dances have 4 beats per measure, so a foxtrot with 30 MPM = 120 BPM. In the tables measures per minute (MPM) is sometimes doubled or halved if that is how the song would be danced.

The third set of tables sort the songs by dance type. If you know what type of dance you want to do, this set of tables may be more useful to you. Even if you don't yet know what type of dance you want to do, as you listen to songs from different categories you will get a sense of the type of sound each dance type has. So, if you really like or dislike the sound of particular dance types you can easily narrow down your choices.

TABLE 1. FIRST DANCE SONGS, SORTED ALPHABETICALLY BY SONG TITLE

Song	Artist	Dance	Speed	MPM	Length
(Everything I Do) I Do It For You	Bryan Adams	Nightclub Two Step or Slow Dance	Ideal	32	6:34
Comments: A pretty song with nice lyrics for a first dance. At about 2:45 in the music, the beat drops out for a few moments - this would be a good place to end the song by fading it out; otherwise dance through that break. Again at about 3:45 to 4:00, the song winds down and sounds like it is over (ideal for ending the dance), then it starts up again, making the song way too long for a First Dance.					
A Groovy Kind Of Love	Phil Collins	Nightclub Two Step	Ideal	36	3:28
Comments: A pretty song with a steady, but soft beat throughout the song.					
A Long and Lasting Love	Crystal Gayle	Rumba	Ideal	29	3:27
Comments: Beautiful lyrics for a first dance. Soft, steady beat throughout song, slows down slightly at very end - which is a great time to do a dip!					
A Love That Will Last	Renee Olstead	Slow Dance	Slow	20	3:31
Comments: A slow-tempo Slow Dance with a soft, jazzy sound. Soft, but clear, steady beat throughout entire song.					

Song	Artist	Dance	Speed	MPM	Length
A Whole New World	Peabo Bryson	Rumba or Slow Dance	Slow	27	4:10

Comments:
A nice rumba, but a little slow. Can also be danced as a Slow Dance. Steady, easy to hear beat until about 3:15, then the beat gets soft and changes tempo. Plan to fade the song by 3:15 (recommended), or be prepared to get creative with your dancing at that point.

Song	Artist	Dance	Speed	MPM	Length
Ain't That Love	Ray Charles	Foxtrot, Swing, or West Coast Swing	Ideal	30	2:51

Comments:
A swingin' song with good lyrics for any of the special dances. The jazzy beat is steady and easy to hear throughout the song with a few hits in the music for the West Coast Swing dancers (which can be ignored for other dances).

Song	Artist	Dance	Speed	MPM	Length
All My Life	K-Ci & JoJo	Rumba	Ideal	32	5:31

Comments:
Sweet lyrics for a first dance. Not the same song as the Linda Ronstadt song by the same name. Steady, easy to hear beat throughout entire song.

Song	Artist	Dance	Speed	MPM	Length
All My Life	Linda Ronstadt	Nightclub Two Step	Ideal	37	3:33

Comments:
Linda Ronstadt featuring Aaron Neville

Not the same song as the K-Ci & JoJo song by the same name. Nice lyrics for a first dance. Steady, easy to hear beat throughout entire song. (Around 2:35, the beat drops out briefly, but the speed remains constant, so you can dance through it, or do a dramatic move at that point, such as a dip.)

Song	Artist	Dance	Speed	MPM	Length
Always And Forever	Heatwave	Viennese Waltz	Ideal	51	6:14

Comments:
Viennese Waltz (advanced dancers) or Hesitation Waltz; Rumba in 6/8 for beginners

Nice lyrics for a first dance. As a Rumba, it is a bit slow and has a non-standard beat, which does make it harder to dance. Hesitation waltz would be the easier dance for this song. There is a short break in the song at about 1:38 and 3:08, but the tempo continues uninterrupted, so you dance through it. The song gets softer around 3:30, then ramps up again after that. We recommend you fade it out by 3 minutes (as with most songs), which will avoid this part of the song. The beat slows down at the very end of the song.

Song	Artist	Dance	Speed	MPM	Length
Amazed	Lonestar	Rumba	Ideal	35	4:00

Comments:
Beautiful lyrics for a first dance. Steady, easy to hear beat throughout the entire song. (Song slows down good slightly after 3:45 as it fades out)

Song	Artist	Dance	Speed	MPM	Length
Anniversary Waltz	Tony Evans And His Orchestra	Waltz	Ideal	31	2:18

Comments:
An old-fashioned sounding waltz with appropriate lyrics for a first dance. Steady, easy to hear beat throughout song.

Song	Artist	Dance	Speed	MPM	Length
Beautiful In My Eyes	Joshua Kadison	Nightclub Two Step	Ideal	35	4:09
Comments: A pretty song with nice lyrics for a First Dance. Steady beat throughout song. The beat is a bit soft for the first minute, then becomes clearer and easier to hear.					
Cheek to Cheek	Ella Fitzgerald & Louis Armstrong	Foxtrot	Ideal	31	5:52
Comments: Nice foxtrot with good lyrics for a First Dance. Steady, easy to hear beat throughout entire song.					
Close to You	The Carpenters	Slow Dance	Ideal	22	3:42
Comments: A love song that could be used for any combination of dancers. Steady, easy to hear beat. There are several breaks in the music where the beat drops out, but the speed is steady, so you can dance through them.					
Colour My World	Chicago	Viennese Waltz	Ideal	53	3:02
Comments: Viennese Waltz (advanced dancers) or Hesitation Waltz; Rumba in 6/8 for beginners Appropriate lyrics for a first dance. As a Rumba, it is a bit slow and has a non-standard beat, which does make it harder to dance. Hesitation waltz would be the easier dance for this song. The beat is steady and easy to hear throughout the entire song.					

Song	Artist	Dance	Speed	MPM	Length
Come By Me	Harry Connick, Jr.	Foxtrot	Fast	39	4:02
Comments: Jazzy fast foxtrot with slightly racy lyrics. Easy to hear beat.					
Could I Have This Dance	Anne Murray	Waltz	Ideal	30	3:16
Comments: Very easy to hear waltz - steady beat throughout entire song (very danceable); great lyrics for wedding first dance. Country song.					
Dance With Me	Anthony Carter	Slow Dance	Ideal	27	3:29
Comments: Dance With Me is a new and refreshing look at the wedding first dance. The lyrics follow the special and intimate moments that a bride and groom experience during their first dance as husband and wife. Instrumental version and sheet music also available. Steady, easy to hear beat throughout entire song (very danceable).					
Endless Love	Anthony Carter	Slow Dance	Ideal	27	3:29
Comments: Beautiful lyrics for a first dance. Steady, but soft, beat throughout song.					
Fascination	Diana Ross & Lionel Ritchie	Slow Dance	Ideal	24	4:29
Comments: A classic waltz with an old fashioned sound. Easy to hear beat.					

Song	Artist	Dance	Speed	MPM	Length
For Once in My Life	Nat King Cole	Waltz	Ideal	29	2:30
Comments: Modern remake of a classic song. More romantic (less jazzy) than the Stevie Wonder version. Steady, easy to hear beat throughout entire song.					
For Once In My Life	Michael Bublé	Slow Dance	Ideal	24	2:33
Comments: A Foxtrot/Swing (which makes it a little difficult because the song is slow), or a Slow Dance (which makes it easier because the tempo/speed is ideal for Slow Dance). Jazzy, steady, easy to hear beat throughout entire song.					
For The First Time	Kenny Loggins	Rumba	Ideal	30	4:28
Comments: Appropriate lyrics for a first dance. Soft, steady beat throughout entire song.					
Forever and Ever, Amen	Randy Travis	Two Step	Ideal	45	3:32
Comments: The lyrics suggest a former bad boy has grown up and is ready to commit for a lifetime. Steady, easy to hear beat throughout entire song.					

Song	Artist	Dance	Speed	MPM	Length
Forever And For Always	Shania Twain	Two Step	Ideal	43	4:43
Comments: Appropriate lyrics for a first dance. Steady, easy to hear beat throughout entire song.					
From This Moment On	Shania Twain	Nightclub Two Step	Ideal	34	4:41
Comments: Long intro (1 minute) with no obvious beat. If you want to use this song, we highly recommend you edit the song to remove the first 60 seconds. After the intro, the beat is clear and steady throughout the rest of the song.					
Give Me Forever (I Do)	John Tesh	Waltz	Ideal	35	3:50
Comments: Beautiful lyrics for a first dance. The beat is hard to hear during the intro (first 20 seconds or so), then is a steady, easy to hear waltz. We suggest swaying romantically to the intro, then switching to waltz when the beat kicks in.					
Grow Old With Me	Mary Chapin Carpenter	Nightclub Two Step	Ideal	37	3:23
Comments: This song has a soft beat which can be challenging to dance to, but the lyrics are sweet for a first dance.					

Song	Artist	Dance	Speed	MPM	Length
Grow Old With You	Adam Sandler	Slow Dance	Ideal	26	1:55

Comments:
Offbeat but fun First Dance song from the movie "The Wedding Singer". Steady, easy to hear beat.

Song	Artist	Dance	Speed	MPM	Length
Have I Told You Lately	Rod Stewart	Nightclub Two Step	Ideal	36	4:01

Comments:
A love song that could be used for any combination of dancers. Steady, easy to hear beat throughout entire song.

Song	Artist	Dance	Speed	MPM	Length
Here And Now	Luther Vandross	Nightclub Two Step	Ideal	35	5:22

Comments:
Beautiful lyrics for a first dance. The beat starts out soft but steady and gets stronger later in the song.

Song	Artist	Dance	Speed	MPM	Length
Here We Stand	Anthony Carter	Rumba	Ideal	30	3:38

Comments:
Here We Stand is a powerful and emotional composition. Written as a unity candle song, but often used as the first dance, Here We Stand captures the precious moments that a bride and groom share before they embark on a new life of togetherness. This original and unique wedding song truly speaks from the heart. Instrumental version and sheet music also available. The beat is steady and clear; there are several breaks in the music but the tempo (speed) remains constant, so you can easily dance through them.

Song	Artist	Dance	Speed	MPM	Length
Hey, Soul Sister	Train	Nightclub Two Step	Ideal	48	3:36
Comments: Upbeat, modern song. Steady, easy to hear beat throughout entire song.					
I Feel So Smoochie	Kurt Elling	Foxtrot	Fast	36	3:18
Comments: Jazzy foxtrot with nice lyrics for a First Dance. Steady beat throughout entire song.					
I Knew I Loved You	Savage Garden	Nightclub Two Step or Slow Dance	Ideal	43	4:11
Comments: Beautiful lyrics for a first dance. It can be danced as a Slow Dance (in half time), or as a fast Nightclub Two Step. Steady, easy to hear beat throughout entire song.					
I Love You	Frank Sinatra	Foxtrot	Ideal	30	2:27
Comments: Appropriate lyrics for a first dance. Steady, easy to hear beat throughout entire song.					

Song	Artist	Dance	Speed	MPM	Length
I Will Always Return [Soundtrack Version (End Title)]	Bryan Adams	Waltz	Ideal	32	2:46

Comments:
A nice waltz with a steady, easy to hear beat throughout entire song. Note that there are two versions of this song on the album. Track 15 is the waltz. Track 2 is a Viennese waltz, which is about twice as fast and is not recommended for beginning dancers.

Song	Artist	Dance	Speed	MPM	Length
I'll Go on Loving You	Alan Jackson	Rumba	Ideal	28	3:57

Comments:
A pretty country song with slightly racy lyrics. Steady, easy to hear beat throughout entire song.

Song	Artist	Dance	Speed	MPM	Length
I'm Sticking with You	The Velvet Underground	Medley	Fast	48; 18; 41	2:28

Comments:
Whimsical lyrics for a First Dance. The first minute is a fast waltz with a clear beat. Then there is no obvious beat from about 1:00 to about 1:25 (be interpretive!). Then the song finishes as a Nightclub Two Step (in double time) or Slow Dance with a clear beat.

Song	Artist	Dance	Speed	MPM	Length
In Your Eyes	Peter Gabriel	Slow Dance	Slow	22	5:27

Comments:
A pretty love song with a steady, easy to hear beat throughout the entire song.

Song	Artist	Dance	Speed	MPM	Length
It Had to Be You	Harry Connick, Jr.	Foxtrot	Ideal	31	2:40

Comments:
A nice foxtrot with decent lyrics for a first dance. Steady, easy to hear beat throughout entire song.

Song	Artist	Dance	Speed	MPM	Length
Kiss From A Rose	Seal	Waltz	Fast	44	4:49

Comments:
A fast waltz with decent lyrics for a first dance. Steady, easy to hear beat. There are several short breaks, but the tempo (speed) is constant, so you can easily dance right through them.

Song	Artist	Dance	Speed	MPM	Length
Let Your Love Flow	The Bellamy Brothers	West Coast Swing or Slow Dance	Ideal	27	3:17

Comments:
A love song with lots of analogies about nature. Steady, easy to hear beat throughout song. Song sounds like it's ending just after 3 minutes, then starts up again at about 3:15. We recommend you end it at this natural ending point.

Song	Artist	Dance	Speed	MPM	Length
Longer	Dan Fogelberg	Slow Dance	Slow	19	3:13

Comments:
A pretty love song with a soft but steady beat throughout entire song.

Song	Artist	Dance	Speed	MPM	Length
Lost In Love	Air Supply	Rumba	Ideal	29	3:52

Comments:
A pretty rumba with nice lyrics for a First Dance and a steady, easy to hear beat throughout entire song.

Song	Artist	Dance	Speed	MPM	Length
L-O-V-E	Natalie Cole	Foxtrot	Fast	38	2:31

Comments:
A fast foxtrot with nice lyrics for a first dance and a steady, easy to hear beat throughout the entire song.

Song	Artist	Dance	Speed	MPM	Length
Love and Marriage	Frank Sinatra	Foxtrot	Ideal	30	2:39

Comments:
A nice foxtrot with good lyrics for a wedding dance. However, this song was used as the theme song of the TV show "Married with Children" (which isn't a very happy portrayal of married life), so keep that in mind if you choose this song. Steady, easy to hear beat throughout the entire song.

Song	Artist	Dance	Speed	MPM	Length
Love Never Fails	Jim Brickman	Nightclub Two Step	Ideal	36	3:45

Comments:
Beautiful lyrics for a first dance. Soft, steady beat throughout entire song.

Song	Artist	Dance	Speed	MPM	Length
Love of a Lifetime	Firehouse	Rumba	Ideal	31	4:46

Comments:
Appropriate lyrics for a first dance. Steady, easy to hear beat throughout entire song.

Song	Artist	Dance	Speed	MPM	Length
Love Of My Life	Jim Brickman	Rumba	Ideal	33	4:00
Comments: Appropriate lyrics for a first dance. Soft beat - slows down and speeds up again a few times, which can be a bit tricky to dance to, especially for beginners.					
Love Song #1	Me'shell Ndegéocello	Rumba	Ideal	35	4:03
Comments: Sexy lyrics - be sure to read them. Beat is not a typical rumba, but is steady and fairly easy to hear.					
Lovin' In My Baby's Eyes	Taj Mahal	Slow Dance	Ideal	21	2:39
Comments: Celebrity choice: Jenna Bush danced her First Dance to this song. It has a steady, easy to hear beat.					
Makes Me Feel This Way	Sara Gazarek	Foxtrot	Ideal	34	3:52
Comments: Jazzy foxtrot with nice lyrics for a First Dance. Steady, easy to hear beat throughout entire song.					

Song	Artist	Dance	Speed	MPM	Length
Making Memories Of Us	Keith Urban	Slow Dance	Ideal	26	4:11

Comments:
Beautiful lyrics for a first dance. Steady, easy to hear beat throughout the entire song.

Moondance	Michael Bublé	Foxtrot	Fast	35	4:13

Comments:
Nice foxtrot with good lyrics for a First Dance. Steady, easy to hear beat throughout entire song. There is one break that can be danced through, and the speed slows down at about 3:30 and fades to end.

More	Bobby Darin	Foxtrot	Fast	37	2:25

Comments:
A fast foxtrot with nice lyrics for a first dance. Steady, easy to hear beat throughout entire song.

My Cup Runneth Over with Love	Ed Ames	Waltz	Ideal	33	2:44

Comments:
An old fashioned waltz with appropriate lyrics for a First Dance. Steady, easy to hear beat throughout entire song.

Song	Artist	Dance	Speed	MPM	Length
My Girl	The Temptations	Slow Dance	Slow	26	2:58

Comments:
A Slow Dance that could be used for a First Dance or Father Daughter Dance. Steady, easy to hear beat throughout entire song.

Song	Artist	Dance	Speed	MPM	Length
Never Had Nobody Like You	M. Ward	West Coast Swing or Rumba	Ideal	30	2:26

Comments:
Slightly offbeat lyrics, expressing gratitude for turning his life around. Steady, easy to hear, swingin' beat with short hits in the music that you can accent in your dance, or dance through, except for a long break from 1:48 to 2:01 where you'll need to do something special (big dip perhaps?) because the beat drops out completely before coming back. You could also end your dance when the big break starts.

Song	Artist	Dance	Speed	MPM	Length
Night and Day	Frank Sinatra	Foxtrot	Ideal	30	4:00

Comments:
Appropriate lyrics for a first dance. Steady, easy to hear beat throughout entire song.

Song	Artist	Dance	Speed	MPM	Length
Now And Forever	Richard Marx	Nightclub Two Step	Ideal	39	3:33

Comments:
A pretty song with a steady, but soft beat throughout the song.

Song	Artist	Dance	Speed	MPM	Length
On the Wings of Love	Jeffrey Osborne	Rumba	Ideal	35	4:04

Comments:
A fast rumba with pretty lyrics for a First Dance. Steady, easy to hear to beat though out entire song.

Song	Artist	Dance	Speed	MPM	Length
One Hand, One Heart	From the Album Forever Mine - Wedding Songs	Waltz	Ideal	34	3:03

Comments:
From the musical "West Side Story". Touching lyrics for a First Dance. There are many recordings of this song - not all of them are easy to dance to. This version is pretty good - the beat is soft, but pretty easy to hear.

Song	Artist	Dance	Speed	MPM	Length
Open Arms	Journey	Waltz	Ideal	34	3:19

Comments:
A decent waltz for dancing - steady beat throughout entire song that starts out soft, then becomes strong and very easy to hear. The lyrics sing of: boy had girl, boy lost girl, boy appreciates having girl back.

Song	Artist	Dance	Speed	MPM	Length
Orange Colored Sky	Natalie Cole	Foxtrot	Ideal	31	2:25

Comments:
A jazzy foxtrot with appropriate lyrics for a First Dance with a steady, easy to hear beat throughout entire song.

Song	Artist	Dance	Speed	MPM	Length
Our Love Is Here To Stay	Frank Sinatra	Foxtrot	Slow	27	2:42
Comments: A slow foxtrot with nice lyrics for a first dance. Steady, soft but clear beat throughout entire song.					
Sea of Love	The Honeydrippers	Slow Dance	Slow	20	3:03
Comments: A slow-tempo Slow Dance with nice lyrics for a First Dance. Clear, steady, easy to hear beat starts at 0:14 and continues throughout the rest of the song. During the intro (first 14 seconds), the beat is hard to hear, so you could just sway in place until the beat kicks in.					
Stand by Me	Ben E. King	Rumba	Ideal	30	2:55
Comments: A pretty rumba that could be used for any of the special dances. Steady, easy to hear beat throughout entire song.					
Sweet Thing	Keith Urban	Two Step	Ideal	51	3:48
Comments: A man reminiscing about his first date and the early days with his Sweet Thing. Steady, easy to hear beat throughout entire song.					

Song	Artist	Dance	Speed	MPM	Length
Take It to The Limit	Eagles	Waltz	Ideal	30	4:46

Comments:
A decent waltz with a steady, easy to hear beat, but questionable lyrics for a First Dance - be sure to read them and decide for yourself.

Song	Artist	Dance	Speed	MPM	Length
Tea-House Moon	Enya	Waltz	Slow	26	2:43

Comments:
A slow, instrumental waltz (no lyrics - so appropriate for any dancers). Steady, easy to hear beat throughout entire song. Because of its slow speed, it can be challenging for beginner dancers.

Song	Artist	Dance	Speed	MPM	Length
The Look Of Love	Diana Krall	Nightclub Two Step or Slow Dance	Ideal	47	4:42

Comments:
Nice lyrics for a first dance. It can be danced as a Slow Dance (in half time), or a fast Nightclub Two Step. Soft, steady beat with a few short breaks that can be danced through.

Song	Artist	Dance	Speed	MPM	Length
The Lover's Waltz Duet	Jay Ungar And Molly Mason	Waltz	Fast	36	3:27

Comments:
Instrumental, easy to hear waltz (no lyrics - so appropriate for any dancers). Soft, steady beat throughout entire song, until 3:00 where the song slows down and fades out.

Song	Artist	Dance	Speed	MPM	Length
The Luckiest	Ben Folds	Rumba	Ideal	31	4:25
Comments: Sweet, though slightly offbeat, lyrics for a First Dance. The beat is a bit hard to hear and slows down a few times, making it potentially challenging to dance to.					
The Prayer	Celine Dion and Andrea Bocelli	Slow Dance	Slow	18	4:27
Comments: Soft beat that can be hard to hear, and very slow - a challenging song to dance to. However, the lyrics are beautiful for a First Dance, or use this song during the wedding ceremony (e.g., lighting the Unity Candle).					
The Sweetheart Tree	Johnny Mathis	Waltz	Slow	28	2:14
Comments: A slow waltz with an old fashioned sound. Steady, easy to hear beat throughout entire song.					
The Way You Look Tonight	Frank Sinatra	Foxtrot	Ideal	30	3:22
Comments: Beautiful, classic wedding dance. Can be used as a First Dance, Father Daughter Dance, or Mother Son Dance. Steady, easy to hear beat throughout entire song (very danceable).					

Song	Artist	Dance	Speed	MPM	Length
The Way You Look Tonight	Michael Bublé	Rumba	Ideal	28	4:37

Comments:
Remake of classic - as a rumba, rather than foxtrot. Steady, easy to hear beat throughout entire song.

Song	Artist	Dance	Speed	MPM	Length
Their Hearts Are Dancing	The Forester Sisters	Waltz	Ideal	33	3:43

Comments:
Very sweet lyrics, although may be more appropriate for an anniversary dance. Steady, soft but clear beat throughout entire song.

Song	Artist	Dance	Speed	MPM	Length
They Can't Take that Away from Me	Frank Sinatra	Foxtrot	Slow	28	1:58

Comments:
A nice foxtrot, but the lyrics are slightly questionable - he sings about possibly never seeing his love again. Steady, easy to hear beat throughout entire song.

Song	Artist	Dance	Speed	MPM	Length
This I Promise You	Journey	Waltz	Ideal	34	3:19

Comments:
Nice lyrics for a First Dance. It can be danced as a Slow Dance (in half time), or a Nightclub Two Step. Steady, easy to hear beat throughout entire song.

Song	Artist	Dance	Speed	MPM	Length
This Ring	Anthony Carter	Rumba	Ideal	28	4:03

Comments:
Brides and grooms are always looking for a new or original song for their wedding first dance. You can't go wrong with choosing This Ring, which is a wedding vow set to beautiful music and truly says it all. Also available as an instrumental version and as sheet music. The beat is very clear except during breaks in the music, which could be a little challenging for beginner dancers to dance through. (Some of the breaks are a little longer than in other songs, which makes them a little challenging.) You could either dance through the breaks, or do something dramatic, like a dip or a romantic kiss, then go right back into dancing when the beat picks up again.

Song	Artist	Dance	Speed	MPM	Length
This Will Be Our Year	The Zombies	Slow Dance	Ideal	25	2:07

Comments:
An upbeat song with a "it was tough but we made it" theme. Steady, easy to hear beat throughout the song (slows down briefly at 1:45, then picks up again and ends).

Song	Artist	Dance	Speed	MPM	Length
Through The Years	Kenny Rogers	Rumba	Ideal	33	4:45

Comments:
A fast rumba with pretty lyrics for a First Dance, especially for a couple that has been together a long time. Often recommended for a Father Daughter or Mother Son Dance, however the lyrics are more about romantic love rather than the love between a parent and child, so keep that in mind. Soft, but steady beat throughout entire song.

Song	Artist	Dance	Speed	MPM	Length
Tonight, I Celebrate My Love	Peabo Bryson with Roberta Flack	Rumba	Ideal	29	3:29

Comments:
A beautiful rumba. The lyrics are about celebrating love by making love. Soft, but steady beat throughout entire song.

Song	Artist	Dance	Speed	MPM	Length
Too Marvelous For Words	Frank Sinatra	Foxtrot	Ideal	32	2:28

Comments:
A nice foxtrot that could be used for a First Dance, Father Daughter Dance, or Mother Son Dance. Steady, easy to hear beat throughout entire song.

Song	Artist	Dance	Speed	MPM	Length
True Companion	Marc Cohn	Rumba or Slow Dance	Ideal	28	4:06

Comments:
Nice lyrics for a First Dance. The intro is 30 seconds long and its beat is hard to hear and drops out - we recommend removing the first 30 seconds. The beat after the intro is soft and still a bit hard to hear - take that into account if you are beginner dancers.

Song	Artist	Dance	Speed	MPM	Length
Truly Madly Deeply	Savage Garden	Nightclub Two Step or Slow Dance	Ideal	42	4:37

Comments:
Nice lyrics for a First Dance. It can be danced as a Slow Dance (in half time), or a Nightclub Two Step. Steady, easy to hear beat throughout entire song.

Song	Artist	Dance	Speed	MPM	Length
Unchained Melody	The Righteous Brothers	Slow Dance, Rumba or Nightclub Two Step in 6/8 timing	Ideal	33	3:36

Comments:
This song can be danced as a rumba or nightclub two step, but the beat is not technically either (the song is in 6/8 instead of 4/4), which makes it more challenging. Slow dance works well and is probably the easiest choice. Steady, easy to hear beat throughout entire song.

Song	Artist	Dance	Speed	MPM	Length
Unforgettable	Natalie Cole and Nat King Cole	Slow Dance	Ideal	21	3:30

Comments:
Lyrics are appropriate for First Dance, Father Daughter Dance, or Mother Son Dance. Soft but steady beat throughout entire song.

Song	Artist	Dance	Speed	MPM	Length
Valentine	Martina McBride and Jim Brickman	Slow Dance	Ideal	24	3:12

Comments:
A pretty love song with nice lyrics for a First Dance and a soft beat that is a little hard to hear at times.

Song	Artist	Dance	Speed	MPM	Length
Wedding Song [There Is Love]	Noel Paul Stookey	Rumba or Foxtrot	Ideal	34	3:46

Comments:
A classic wedding song with religious overtones. Can be danced as a rumba (our preference) or foxtrot. Steady, easy to hear beat throughout entire song.

Song	Artist	Dance	Speed	MPM	Length
When I Fall In Love	Céline Dion and Clive Griffin	Nightclub Two Step or Slow Dance	Ideal	36	4:21

Comments:
A pretty song with a steady, but soft beat throughout the song until the very end when it slows down.

Song	Artist	Dance	Speed	MPM	Length
When I Need You	Leo Sayer	Waltz	Fast	36	4:13

Comments:
A fast waltz. Lyrics are about a man who is traveling and missing his sweetheart. Beat very hard to hear during intro (first 26 seconds), then is soft but steady throughout remainder of song.

Song	Artist	Dance	Speed	MPM	Length
With You I'm Born Again	Vanessa Williams and George Benson	Waltz	Slow	27	3:53

Comments:
A slow waltz with pretty lyrics. The beat during the first 2 minutes of the song is pretty soft and can be hard to hear. After 2 minutes, the gets stronger and easier to hear until about 3:15 where the song starts to slow down and the beat gets softer again.

Song	Artist	Dance	Speed	MPM	Length
Wonderful, Wonderful	Johnny Mathis	Foxtrot	Fast	36	2:50

Comments:
A fast foxtrot with nice lyrics for a first dance. Steady, easy to hear beat throughout entire song.

Song	Artist	Dance	Speed	MPM	Length
You & Me	Dave Matthews Band	Slow Dance	Ideal	23	5:40

Comments:
Nice song about spending your lives together. The music is a bit more complex than other songs, making the beat harder to hear sometimes (e.g., the first minute).

Song	Artist	Dance	Speed	MPM	Length
You Are My Sunshine	Sara Gazarek	Foxtrot	Ideal	30	3:34

Comments:
Jazzy foxtrot version of a classic. This song is often recommended for a First Dance, and more traditional versions of the song include parts that aren't a good fit in our opinion. For example "But now you've left me and love another..." Sara Gazarek's version, however, leaves that verse out, making it far more appropriate for a wedding. The beat is generally steady and easy to hear, except for a few short breaks which could be a little hard to hear but are easy enough to dance through.

Song	Artist	Dance	Speed	MPM	Length
You Light Up My Life	Whitney Houston	Waltz	Ideal	31	3:41

Comments:
Many artists have performed this classic song. Most of them are easy to hear and dance to (including this one), so pick your favorite.

Song	Artist	Dance	Speed	MPM	Length
You Make Me Feel Like A Natural Woman	Aretha Franklin	Waltz	Ideal	35	2:47

Comments:
The lyrics are ok for a First Dance. The beat is steady and pretty easy to hear throughout the song.

Song	Artist	Dance	Speed	MPM	Length
You Make Me Feel So Young	Frank Sinatra	Foxtrot	Ideal	31	2:56

Comments:
A happy song with a steady, easy-to-hear beat throughout entire song.

Song	Artist	Dance	Speed	MPM	Length
You Raise Me Up	Josh Groban	Slow Dance	Ideal	28	4:01

Comments:
A slow dance with a beautiful message about love. Good for a First Dance, and especially good for a Father Daughter or Mother Son dance. Beat alternates between soft (not super easy to hear) and very clear and easy to hear.

Song	Artist	Dance	Speed	MPM	Length
You're Still The One	Shania Twain	Rumba	Ideal	33	3:32

Comments:
A beautiful rumba with lyrics about enduring love - especially good for couples who have been together a long time. Steady, easy to hear beat throughout entire song.

Song	Artist	Dance	Speed	MPM	Length
You're My Best Friend	Queen	Foxtrot	Ideal	30	2:50

Comments:
A nice foxtrot with decent lyrics for a first dance. Steady, easy to hear beat throughout entire song.

Song	Artist	Dance	Speed	MPM	Length
You're Nobody 'Til Somebody Loves You	Dean Martin	Foxtrot	Ideal	32	2:12

Comments:
A nice foxtrot with ok lyrics for a first dance. Steady, easy to hear beat throughout entire song.

Song	Artist	Dance	Speed	MPM	Length
You're The Inspiration	Chicago	Nightclub Two Step	Ideal	38	3:47

Comments:
Nice lyrics for a First Dance. Beat alternates between very clear (easy to hear) and a bit soft (harder to hear).

TABLE 2. FATHER-DAUGHTER AND MOTHER-SON SONGS, SORTED ALPHABETICALLY BY SONG TITLE

(Note: F-D refers to Father-Daughter Dance and M-S refers to Mother-Son Dance.)

Song	Artist	Dance	Speed	MPM	Length	F-D	M-S
A Mother's Song	Anthony Carter	Rumba	Ideal	30	3:34		✓
Comments: A Mother's Song captures the loving bond between a mother and her son. With lyrics from little boy days to his most special day, this song is sure to tug at the heartstrings of all who listen. A new favorite among mother son wedding songs. Instrumental version and sheet music also available. "Tying little shoe laces, wiping off dirty faces are just a couple of things that a mother will do…"							
A Song For Mama	Boyz II Men	Nightclub Two Step	Ideal	37	5:03		✓
Comments: A song about a son's love for his mother. "You taught me everything, and everything you've given me - I always keep it inside…"							

Song	Artist	Dance	Speed	MPM	Length	F-D	M-S
A Song For My Daughter	Mikki Viereck OR Ray Allaire	Rumba	Ideal	32	3:39	✓	

Comments:
A Song For My Daughter is the second CD single release from New Traditions following the very successful A Song For My Son - the first song in history ever written for the mother and groom dance at a wedding reception. The CD single of A Song For My Daughter contains both a male vocal version (Ray Allaire) and a female vocal version (Mikki Viereck), so the song can be either from the father to the bride or from the mother to the bride.
"Just once upon a yesterday I held you in my arms; you grew into a little girl with lovely childhood charms…"

Song	Artist	Dance	Speed	MPM	Length	F-D	M-S
A Song for My Son (Traditional OR Country version)	Mikki Viereck OR Donna Lee Honeywell	Waltz	Fast OR Ideal	38 OR 33	3:05		✓

Comments:
A beautiful song about a mother's feelings toward her son on his wedding day. Have kleenex ready when listening to this song. The traditional version (by Mikki Viereck) is faster than the country version (by Donna Lee Honeywell). Both versions are waltzes that are very danceable and moving.
"I don't know where the time has gone since those little boy days …"

Song	Artist	Dance	Speed	MPM	Length	F-D	M-S
Ain't That Love	Ray Charles	Foxtrot	Ideal	30	2:51	✓	✓

Comments:
A nice-tempo foxtrot with good lyrics for any of the special dances.
"Now, baby when you sigh (when you sigh) I wanna sigh with you…"

Song	Artist	Dance	Speed	MPM	Length	F-D	M-S
Because You Loved Me	Celine Dion	Rumba	Ideal	30	4:33	✓	✓

Comments:
Touching lyrics for a Father Daughter or Mother Son dance.
"For all those times you stood by me for all the truth that you made me see…"

Song	Artist	Dance	Speed	MPM	Length	F-D	M-S
Blessed	Elton John	Slow Dance	Ideal	25	4:22	✓	✓

Comments:
Sweet lyrics about a parent's love before the child was even born.
"Hey you, you're a child in my head - you haven't walked yet, your first words have yet to be said - but I swear you'll be blessed …"

Song	Artist	Dance	Speed	MPM	Length	F-D	M-S
Butterfly Kisses	Bob Carlisle	Nightclub Two Step or Slow Dance	Ideal	40	5:38	✓	

Comments:
Very touching lyrics for a Father Daughter dance. It can be danced as a Slow Dance (in half time), or a fast Nightclub Two Step.

"There's two things I know for sure: she was sent here from heaven and she's daddy's little girl…"

Song	Artist	Dance	Speed	MPM	Length	F-D	M-S
Can You Feel The Love Tonight	Elton John	Rumba	Ideal	30	4:00	✓	✓

Comments:
A love song that could be used for any combination of dancers.
"There's a calm surrender to the rush of day when the heat of a rolling wind can be turned away"

Song	Artist	Dance	Speed	MPM	Length	F-D	M-S
Child Of Mine	Carole King	Nightclub Two Step	Ideal	33	3:43	✓	✓

Comments:
Touching lyrics for a Father Daughter or Mother Son dance.
"Although you see the world different than me, sometimes I can touch upon the wonders that you see..."

Song	Artist	Dance	Speed	MPM	Length	F-D	M-S
Close to You	The Carpenters	Slow Dance	Ideal	22	3:42	✓	✓

Comments:
A love song that could be used for any combination of dancers.
"Why do birds suddenly appear every time you are near?"

Song	Artist	Dance	Speed	MPM	Length	F-D	M-S
Daddy's Angel	Anthony Carter	Nightclub Two Step	Ideal	37	3:52	✓	

Comments:
Daddy's Angel shares all of the words that a father wants to say to his daughter on her wedding day. With lyrics that capture childhood memories and special moments that last forever, Daddy's Angel speaks from a father's heart. Instrumental version and sheet music also available.
"I'm giving you away, but I'm not letting go, the memories, they flood my mind of the little girl I know …"

Song	Artist	Dance	Speed	MPM	Length	F-D	M-S
Daddy's Hands	Holly Dunn	Two Step	Slow	38	3:29	✓	

Comments:
The song is a bit slow for a CW Two Step (although still danceable). Nightclub Two Step (ideal speed) or Foxtrot (fast) would also work
"I remember Daddy's hands folded silently in prayer, and reaching out to hold me when I had a nightmare…"

Song	Artist	Dance	Speed	MPM	Length	F-D	M-S
Daddy's Little Girl	Al Martino	Waltz	Ideal	30	2:32	✓	

Comments:
An easy waltz with very sweet lyrics for a Father Daughter dance.
"You're Daddy's Little Girl, you're the end of the rainbow - my Pot of Gold…"

Song	Artist	Dance	Speed	MPM	Length	F-D	M-S
Dance With My Father	Celine Dion or Luther Vandross	Nightclub Two Step or Slow Dance	Ideal	41	4:38	✓	

Comments:
Although this song is commonly suggested for Father Daughter dances, it is actually a child's tribute to his/her father who has passed away, asking the Lord to send him back to them (the child and his mother). It can be danced as a Slow Dance (in half time), or a fast Nightclub Two Step.
"Back when I was a child before life removed all the innocence, my father would lift me high…"

Song	Artist	Dance	Speed	MPM	Length	F-D	M-S
Daughter	Loudon Wain-wright III	Nightclub Two Step	Ideal	45	3:34	✓	

Comments:
A father singing about his daughter.
"Everything she sees she says she wants. Everything she wants I see she gets…."

Song	Artist	Dance	Speed	MPM	Length	F-D	M-S
Father And Daughter	Paul Simon	Slow Dance	Ideal	27	4:10	✓	

Comments:
The chorus is great; the verses are a little odd here and there - check it out for yourself.
"If you ever leap awake In the mirror of a bad dream…"

Song	Artist	Dance	Speed	MPM	Length	F-D	M-S
Good-night, Demon-slayer	Voltaire	Waltz	Fast	41	4:49	✓	✓

Comments:
Parent to child, addressing childhood fears about demons under the bed at night. Whimsical choice for a Parent Child dance.
"There's a monster that lives 'neath your bed, oh for crying out loud it's a futon on the floor..."

Song	Artist	Dance	Speed	MPM	Length	F-D	M-S
Have I Told You Lately	Rod Stewart	Nightclub Two Step	Ideal	36	4:01	✓	✓

Comments:
A love song that could be used for any combination of dancers.
"I told you lately that I love you; have I told you there's no one else above you..."

Song	Artist	Dance	Speed	MPM	Length	F-D	M-S
Here for You	Neil Young	Slow Dance	Ideal	27	4:29	✓	✓

Comments:
Nice lyrics for either a Father Daughter or Mother Son Dance
"When your summer days come tumbling down and you find yourself alone ..."

Song	Artist	Dance	Speed	MPM	Length	F-D	M-S
Hero	Mariah Carey	Rumba	Ideal	30	4:19		✓

Comments:
A pretty song with lyrics that work for a Mother Son dance.
"There's a hero if you look inside your heart, you don't have to be afraid of what you are..."

Song	Artist	Dance	Speed	MPM	Length	F-D	M-S
I Am Your Child	Barry Manilow	Rumba	Ideal	31	2:18	✓	✓
Comments: Appropriate lyrics for a Father Daughter or Mother Son dance. We recommend you dance rumba in double time (1&2 3&4), which makes for a nice tempo. "I am your child, wherever you go, you take me, too, whatever I know, I learn from you…"							
I Can See Clearly Now	Johnny Nash	Rumba	Ideal	31	2:55	✓	✓
Comments: A happy song with an easy-to-hear beat. "I can see clearly now, the rain is gone, I can see all obstacles in my way…"							
Isn't She Lovely	Stevie Wonder	Rumba	Ideal	30	6:34	✓	
Comments: A pretty song song by a man about his baby daughter "Isn't she lovely, isn't she wonderful, isn't she precious, less than one minute old…"							
Kind and Generous	Natalie Merchant	Slow Dance	Ideal	23	4:01	✓	✓
Comments: A song about gratitude "You've been so kind and generous, I don't know how you keep on giving…"							

Song	Artist	Dance	Speed	MPM	Length	F-D	M-S
Lean on Me	Bill Withers	Nightclub Two Step	Ideal	37	4:17	✓	✓
Comments: A song that works for either Father Daughter or Mother Son dances "Sometimes in our lives we all have pain, we all have sorrow, but if we are wise, we know that there's always tomorrow…"							
Let There Be Love	Oasis	Nightclub Two Step	Ideal	37	5:31	✓	✓
Comments: A song that works for either Father Daughter or Mother Son dances "Who kicked a hole in the sky so the heavens would cry over me?…"							
Let Your Love Flow	The Bellamy Brothers	West Coast Swing or Slow Dance	Ideal	27	3:17	✓	✓
Comments: A love song with lots of analogies about nature "There's a reason for the sun shiny sky, and there's a reason why I'm feelin' so high…"							
Loves Me Like a Rock	Paul Simon	Swing	Ideal	36	3:32		✓
Comments: Something a little different for a Mother Son dance – an upbeat swing. "When I was a little boy (when I was just a boy), and the Devil would call my name (when I was just a boy)…"							

Song	Artist	Dance	Speed	MPM	Length	F-D	M-S
Lullaby (Good Night My Angel)	Billy Joel	Nightclub Two Step	Ideal	38	3:34	✓	

Comments:
A pretty song for a Father Daughter dance
"Good night my angel time to close you eyes and save these questions for another day..."

Song	Artist	Dance	Speed	MPM	Length	F-D	M-S
Mama	B. J. Thomas	Waltz	Ideal	32	2:59		✓

Comments:
Country waltz with easy to hear beat and sweet lyrics for a Mother Son Dance.
"Who's the one who tied your shoe when you were young and knew just when to come and see what you had done...?"

Song	Artist	Dance	Speed	MPM	Length	F-D	M-S
Memories	Elvis Presley	Slow Dance	Ideal	22	3:05		✓

Comments:
A pretty, sentimental song
"Memories, pressed between the pages of my mind; memories, sweetened through the ages just like wine..."

Song	Artist	Dance	Speed	MPM	Length	F-D	M-S
My Girl	The Temp-tations	Slow Dance	Ideal	26	2:58	✓	

Comments:
A Slow Dance that could be used for a First Dance or Father Daughter Dance.
"I've got sunshine on a cloudy day. When it's cold outside I've got the month of May..."

Song	Artist	Dance	Speed	MPM	Length	F-D	M-S
My Little Girl (from My Friend Flicka)	Tim McGraw	Nightclub Two Step	Ideal	36	3:40	✓	
Comments: Very sweet lyrics for a Father Daughter Dance. "Gotta hold on easy as I let you go, gonna tell you how much I love you, though you think you already know..."							
Samba Pa' Ti	Santana	Samba/ Bossa Nova	Slow	41	4:45	✓	✓
Comments: A lazy Samba. Instrumental (no lyrics)							
Song for My Son (Maybe You'll Never Know)	Winsome	Slow Dance	Ideal	27	3:25		✓
Comments: A mother singing about her love for her son over time. "You're in my heart now I just have to say, there's a love for you and it won't go away..."							
Stand by Me	Ben E. King	Rumba	Ideal	30	2:55	✓	✓
Comments: A pretty rumba that could be used for any of the special dances "When the night has come, and the land is dark, and the moon is the only light we'll see..."							

Song	Artist	Dance	Speed	MPM	Length	F-D	M-S
Sunrise, Sunset	Complete Wedding Music Resource	Waltz	Ideal	35	4:15	✓	✓
Comments: This is a old-fashioned waltz with sweet lyrics for a Father Daughter or Mother Son Dance. Many versions of the song are easy to hear the beat. We recommend this version. "Is this the little girl I carried? Is this the little boy at play? I don't remember growing older When did they?..."							
Tea-House Moon	Enya	Waltz	Slow	26	2:43	✓	✓
Comments: A slow, instrumental waltz (no lyrics - so appropriate for any dancers)							
Thank Heaven for Little Girls	Merle Haggard	Foxtrot	Fast	35	2:31	✓	
Comments: Sweet lyrics for a Father Daughter Dance "Thank heaven for little girls, for little girls get bigger every day..."							
The Earth, The Sun, The Rain	Color Me Badd	Nightclub Two Step	Ideal	39	4:16		✓
Comments: A pretty song for a Mother Son dance "When I was lost, I could not see all the beauty and wonder, wrapping around me..."							

Song	Artist	Dance	Speed	MPM	Length	F-D	M-S
The Lover's Waltz	Jay Ungar And Molly Mason	Waltz	Fast	36	3:27	✓	✓

Comments:
Instrumental, easy to hear waltz (no lyrics - so appropriate for any dancers)

Song	Artist	Dance	Speed	MPM	Length	F-D	M-S
The Way You Look Tonight	Frank Sinatra	Foxtrot	Ideal	30	3:22	✓	✓

Comments:
Beautiful, classic wedding dance. Can be used as a First Dance, Father Daughter Dance, or Mother Son Dance.
"Someday, when I'm awfully low, when the world is cold..."

Song	Artist	Dance	Speed	MPM	Length	F-D	M-S
The Way You Look Tonight	Michael Bublé	Rumba	Ideal	28	4:37	✓	✓

Comments:
Remake of classic - as rumba, rather than foxtrot. More modern sound. (Could also be danced as a foxtrot.)
"Someday, when I'm awfully low, when the world is cold..."

Song	Artist	Dance	Speed	MPM	Length	F-D	M-S
There You'll Be	Faith Hill	Rumba	Ideal	32	3:40	✓	✓

Comments:
Nice lyrics for either a Father Daughter or Mother Son Dance
"When I think back on these times and the dreams we left behind, I'll be glad 'cause I was blessed to get to have you in my life ..."

Song	Artist	Dance	Speed	MPM	Length	F-D	M-S
Through The Years	Kenny Rogers	Rumba	Ideal	33	4:45	✓	

Comments:
A fast rumba with pretty lyrics for a First Dance, especially for a couple that has been together a long time. Sometimes recommended for a Father Daughter or Mother Son Dance, but the lyrics are more about romantic love rather than the love between a parent and child.
"I can't remember when you weren't there, when I didn't care for anyone but you…"

Song	Artist	Dance	Speed	MPM	Length	F-D	M-S
Times of Your Life	Paul Anka	Nightclub Two Step	Ideal	38	3:12	✓	✓

Comments:
A sentimental song about memories for a Parent Child Dance
"Good morning, yesterday, you wake up and time has slipped away…"

Song	Artist	Dance	Speed	MPM	Length	F-D	M-S
Too Marvelous For Words	Frank Sinatra	Foxtrot	Ideal	32	2:28	✓	✓

Comments:
A nice foxtrot that could be used for a First Dance, Father Daughter Dance, or Mother Son Dance.
"You're just too marvelous, too marvelous for words, like "glorious", "glamorous" and that old standby "amorous"…"

Song	Artist	Dance	Speed	MPM	Length	F-D	M-S
Turn Around	Perry Como	Waltz	Ideal	31	2:30	✓	

Comments:
Many others have also recorded this song. Unlike some other versions, Perry Como's version has an easy to hear beat.
"Turnaround, turnaround, turnaround and you're a young girl going out of the door…"

Song	Artist	Dance	Speed	MPM	Length	F-D	M-S
Unfor-gettable	Natalie Cole and Nat King Cole	Slow Dance	Ideal	21	3:30	✓	✓

Comments:
Lyrics are appropriate for First Dance, Father Daughter Dance, or Mother Son Dance.
"Unforgettable, that's what you are. Unforgettable, though near or far…"

Song	Artist	Dance	Speed	MPM	Length	F-D	M-S
Universe & U	KT Tun-stall	Nightclub Two Step	Ideal	33	4:01	✓	✓

Comments:
A song that works for either Father Daughter or Mother Son dances
"A fire burns, water comes, you cool me down when I'm cold inside, you are warm and bright…"

Song	Artist	Dance	Speed	MPM	Length	F-D	M-S
What A Wonderful World	Louis Arm-strong	Nightclub Two Step	Ideal	36	2:20	✓	✓

Comments:
This song is in 6/8 (which means nothing to you if you don't know anything about music, and that's ok), but it works well as a Nightclub Two Step anyway.
"I see trees of green, red roses too, I see them bloom for me and you…"

Song	Artist	Dance	Speed	MPM	Length	F-D	M-S
What The World Needs Now Is Love	Jackie Deshannon	Waltz	Fast	36	3:15	✓	✓
Comments: A fast waltz with nice lyrics "What the world needs now, is love, sweet love, it's the only thing that there's just too little of…"							
Wind Beneath My Wings	Bette Midler	Rumba	Ideal	31	4:55	✓	✓
Comments: A nice rumba with lyrics that are especially good for a Mother Son Dance, although they could work for a Father Daughter Dance too. "It must have been cold there in my shadow, to never have sunlight on your face…"							
You Are So Beautiful	Joe Cocker	Rumba	Ideal	31	2:42	✓	✓
Comments: A pretty rumba that could be used for any of the special dances "You are so beautiful to me, can't you see? You're everything I hoped for …"							

Song	Artist	Dance	Speed	MPM	Length	F-D	M-S
You Are The Sunshine Of My Life	Stevie Wonder	Rumba	Ideal	32	2:50	✓	✓

Comments:
A nice-tempo foxtrot or rumba with good lyrics for any of the special dances "You are the sunshine of my life, that's why I'll always be around…"

Song	Artist	Dance	Speed	MPM	Length	F-D	M-S
You Raise Me Up	Josh Groban	Slow Dance	Ideal	28	4:01	✓	✓

Comments:
A slow dance with a beautiful message about love. Good for a First Dance, and especially good for a Parent Child dance. "When I am down and, oh my soul, so weary; When troubles come and my heart burdened be…"

Song	Artist	Dance	Speed	MPM	Length	F-D	M-S
You've Got A Friend	James Taylor	Nightclub Two Step or Slow Dance	Ideal	46	4:30	✓	✓

Comments:
Ok lyrics for a Parent Child dance. It can be danced as a Slow Dance (in half time), or a fast Nightclub Two Step. "When your down and troubled and you need a helping hand, and nothing, whoa nothing is going right…"

TABLE 3A. FOXTROT

First Dance and Parent Child Songs

(Note: F-D refers to Father-Daughter Dance and M-S refers to Mother-Son Dance.)

Song	Artist	Dance	Speed MPM Length	F-D	M-S	First Dance
Ain't That Love	Ray Charles	Foxtrot, Swing, or West Coast Swing	Ideal 30 2:51	✓	✓	✓
Cheek to Cheek	Ella Fitzgerald & Louis Armstrong	Foxtrot	Ideal 31 5:52			✓
Come By Me	Harry Connick, Jr.	Foxtrot	Fast 39 4:02			✓
For Once In My Life	Stevie Wonder	Foxtrot, Swing, or Slow Dance	Slow or Ideal 27 2:50			✓
I Feel So Smoochie	Kurt Elling	Foxtrot	Fast 36 3:18			✓
I Love You	Frank Sinatra	Foxtrot	Ideal 30 2:27			✓

Song	Artist	Dance	Speed MPM Length	F-D	M-S	First Dance
It Had to Be You	Harry Connick, Jr.	Foxtrot	Ideal 31 2:40			✓
L-O-V-E	Natalie Cole	Foxtrot	Fast 38 2:31			✓
Love and Marriage	Frank Sinatra	Foxtrot	Ideal 30 2:39			✓
Makes Me Feel This Way	Sara Gazarek	Foxtrot	Ideal 34 3:52			✓
Moondance	Michael Bublé	Foxtrot	Fast 35 4:13			✓
More	Bobby Darin	Foxtrot	Fast 37 2:25			✓
Night and Day	Frank Sinatra	Foxtrot	Ideal 30 4:00			✓
Orange Colored Sky	Natalie Cole	Foxtrot	Ideal 31 2:25			✓
Our Love Is Here To Stay	Frank Sinatra	Foxtrot	Slow 27 2:42			✓

Song	Artist	Dance	Speed MPM Length	F-D	M-S	First Dance
Thank Heaven for Little Girls	Merle Haggard	Foxtrot	Fast 35 2:31	✓		
The Way You Look Tonight	Frank Sinatra	Foxtrot	Ideal 30 3:22	✓	✓	✓
They Can't Take that Away from Me	Frank Sinatra	Foxtrot	Slow 28 1:58			✓
Too Marvelous For Words	Frank Sinatra	Foxtrot	Ideal 32 2:28	✓	✓	✓
Wedding Song [There Is Love]	Noel Paul Stookey	Rumba or Foxtrot	Ideal 34 3:46			✓
Wonderful, Wonderful	Johnny Mathis	Foxtrot	Fast 36 2:50			✓
You Are My Sunshine	Sara Gazarek	Foxtrot	Ideal 30 3:34			✓
You Are The Sunshine Of My Life	Stevie Wonder	Rumba or Foxtrot	Ideal 32 2:50			✓

Song	Artist	Dance	Speed MPM Length	F-D	M-S	First Dance
You Make Me Feel So Young	Frank Sinatra	Foxtrot	Ideal 31 2:56			✓
You're My Best Friend	Queen	Foxtrot	Ideal 30 2:50			✓
You're Nobody 'Til Somebody Loves You	Dean Martin	Foxtrot	Ideal 32 2:12			✓

TABLE 3B. NIGHTCLUB TWO STEP

First Dance and Parent Child Songs

Note that Two Step (a country dance) and Nightclub Two Step (a "love song" dance) are completely different dances.

(Note: F-D refers to Father-Daughter Dance and M-S refers to Mother-Son Dance.)

Song	Artist	Dance	Speed MPM Length	F-D	M-S	First Dance
(Everything I Do) I Do It For You	Bryan Adams	Nightclub Two Step or Slow Dance	Ideal 32 6:34			✓
A Groovy Kind Of Love	Phil Collins	Nightclub Two Step	Ideal 36 3:28			✓
All My Life	Linda Ronstadt featuring Aaron Neville	Nightclub Two Step	Ideal 37 3:33			✓
A Song For Mama	Boyz II Men	Nightclub Two Step	Ideal 37 5:03		✓	
Beautiful In My Eyes	Joshua Kadison	Nightclub Two Step	Ideal 35 4:09			✓
Blood of Eden	Peter Gabriel	Nightclub Two Step	Ideal 40 5:07			✓

Song	Artist	Dance	Speed MPM Length	F-D	M-S	First Dance
Butterfly Kisses	Bob Carlisle	Nightclub Two Step or Slow Dance	Ideal 40 5:38	✓		
Child Of Mine	Carole King	Nightclub Two Step	Ideal 33 3:43	✓	✓	
Daddy's Angel	Anthony Carter	Nightclub Two Step	Ideal 37 3:52	✓		
Dance With My Father	Celine Dion or Luther Vandross	Nightclub Two Step or Slow Dance	Ideal 41 4:38	✓		
Daughter	Loudon Wainwright III	Nightclub Two Step	Ideal 45 3:34	✓		
From This Moment On	Shania Twain	Nightclub Two Step	Ideal 34 4:41			✓
Grow Old With Me	Mary Chapin Carpenter	Nightclub Two Step	Ideal 37 3:23			✓
Have I Told You Lately	Rod Stewart	Nightclub Two Step	Ideal 36 4:01	✓	✓	✓
Here And Now	Luther Vandross	Nightclub Two Step	Ideal 35 5:22			✓

Song	Artist	Dance	Speed MPM Length	F-D	M-S	First Dance
Hey, Soul Sister	Train	Nightclub Two Step	Ideal 48 3:36			✓
I Knew I Loved You	Savage Garden	Nightclub Two Step or Slow Dance	Ideal 43 4:11			✓
Lean on Me	Bill Withers	Nightclub Two Step	Ideal 37 4:17	✓	✓	
Let There Be Love	Oasis	Nightclub Two Step	Ideal 37 5:31	✓	✓	
Love Never Fails	Jim Brickman	Nightclub Two Step	Ideal 36 3:45			✓
Lullaby (Good Night My Angel)	Billy Joel	Nightclub Two Step	Ideal 38 3:34	✓		
Over the Rainbow	Israel "IZ" Kamakawiwo'ole	Nightclub Two Step	Ideal 42 3:31	✓	✓	
My Little Girl (from My Friend Flicka)	Tim McGraw	Nightclub Two Step	Ideal 36 3:40	✓		
Now And Forever	Richard Marx	Nightclub Two Step	Ideal 39 3:33			✓

Song	Artist	Dance	Speed MPM Length	F-D	M-S	First Dance
The Earth, The Sun, The Rain	Color Me Badd	Nightclub Two Step	Ideal 39 4:16		✓	
The Look Of Love	Diana Krall	Nightclub Two Step or Slow Dance	Ideal 47 4:42			✓
This I Promise You	N Sync	Nightclub Two Step or Slow Dance	Ideal 42 4:26			✓
Times of Your Life	Paul Anka	Nightclub Two Step	Ideal 38 3:12	✓	✓	
Truly Madly Deeply	Savage Garden	Nightclub Two Step or Slow Dance	Ideal 42 4:37			✓
Unchained Melody	The Righteous Brothers	Slow Dance, Rumba or Nightclub Two Step in 6/8 timing	Ideal 33 3:36			✓
Universe & U	KT Tunstall	Nightclub Two Step	Ideal 33 4:01	✓	✓	

Song	Artist	Dance	Speed MPM Length	F-D	M-S	First Dance
What A Wonderful World	Louis Armstrong	Nightclub Two Step	Ideal 36 2:20	✓	✓	
When I Fall In Love	Céline Dion and Clive Griffin	Nightclub Two Step or Slow Dance	Ideal 36 4:21			✓
You're The Inspiration	Chicago	Nightclub Two Step	Ideal 38 3:47			✓
You've Got A Friend	James Taylor	Nightclub Two Step or Slow Dance	Ideal 46 4:30	✓	✓	

TABLE 3C. RUMBA

First Dance and Parent Child Songs

(Note: F-D refers to Father-Daughter Dance and M-S refers to Mother-Son Dance.)

Song	Artist	Dance	Speed MPM Length	F-D	M-S	First Dance
A Long and Lasting Love	Crystal Gayle	Rumba	Ideal 29 3:27			✓
A Whole New World	Peabo Bryson	Rumba or Slow Dance	Slow 27 4:10			✓
All My Life	K-Ci & JoJo	Rumba	Ideal 32 5:31			✓
Always And Forever	Heatwave	Rumba in 6/8 for beginners	Ideal 51 6:14			✓
Amazed	Lonestar	Rumba	Ideal 35 4:00			✓
A Mother's Song	Anthony Carter	Rumba	Ideal 30 3:34		✓	
A Song For My Daughter	Mikki Viereck OR Ray Allaire	Rumba	Ideal 32 3:39	✓		
Because You Loved Me	Celine Dion	Rumba	Ideal 30 4:33	✓	✓	

Song	Artist	Dance	Speed MPM Length	F-D	M-S	First Dance
Can You Feel The Love Tonight	Elton John	Rumba	Ideal 30 4:00	✓	✓	✓
Colour My World	Chicago	Rumba in 6/8 for beginners	Ideal 53 3:02			✓
For The First Time	Kenny Loggins	Rumba	Ideal 30 4:28			✓
For You I Will	Monica	Rumba	Ideal 31 4:54			✓
Here We Stand	Anthony Carter	Rumba	Ideal 30 3:38			✓
Hero	Mariah Carey	Rumba	Ideal 30 4:19		✓	
I Am Your Child	Barry Manilow	Rumba	Ideal 31 2:18	✓	✓	
I Can See Clearly Now	Johnny Nash	Rumba	Ideal 31 2:55	✓	✓	
I'll Go on Loving You	Alan Jackson	Rumba	Ideal 28 3:57			✓

Song	Artist	Dance	Speed MPM Length	F-D	M-S	First Dance
Isn't She Lovely	Stevie Wonder	Rumba	Ideal 30 6:34	✓		
Lost In Love	Air Supply	Rumba	Ideal 29 3:52			✓
Love of a Lifetime	Firehouse	Rumba	Ideal 31 4:46			✓
Love Of My Life	Jim Brickman	Rumba	Ideal 33 4:00			✓
Love Song #1	Me'shell Ndegéocello	Rumba	Ideal 35 4:03			✓
Never Had Nobody Like You	M. Ward	West Coast Swing or Rumba	Ideal 30 2:26			✓
On the Wings of Love	Jeffrey Osborne	Rumba	Ideal 35 4:04			✓
Stand by Me	Ben E. King	Rumba	Ideal 30 2:55	✓	✓	✓
The Luckiest	Ben Folds	Rumba	Ideal 31 4:25			✓

Song	Artist	Dance	Speed MPM Length	F-D	M-S	First Dance
There You'll Be	Faith Hill	Rumba	Ideal 32 3:40	✓	✓	
The Way You Look Tonight	Michael Bublé	Rumba	Ideal 28 4:37	✓	✓	✓
This Ring	Anthony Carter	Rumba	Ideal 28 4:03			✓
Through The Years	Kenny Rogers	Rumba	Ideal 33 4:45	✓	✓	✓
Tonight, I Celebrate My Love	Peabo Bryson with Roberta Flack	Rumba	Ideal 29 3:29			✓
True Companion	Marc Cohn	Rumba or Slow Dance	Ideal 28 4:06			✓
Unchained Melody	The Righteous Brothers	Slow Dance, Rumba or Nightclub Two Step in 6/8 timing	Ideal 33 3:36			✓
Wedding Song [There Is Love]	Noel Paul Stookey	Rumba or Foxtrot	Ideal 34 3:46			✓

Song	Artist	Dance	Speed MPM Length	F-D	M-S	First Dance
Wind Beneath My Wings	Bette Midler	Rumba	Ideal 31 4:55	✓	✓	
You Are So Beautiful	Joe Cocker	Rumba	Ideal 31 2:42	✓	✓	✓
You Are The Sunshine Of My Life	Stevie Wonder	Rumba or Foxtrot	Ideal 32 2:50	✓	✓	✓
You're Still The One	Shania Twain	Rumba	Ideal 33 3:32			✓

TABLE 3D. SAMBA/BOSSA NOVA

First Dance and Parent Child Songs
(Note: F-D refers to Father-Daughter Dance and M-S refers to Mother-Son Dance.)

Song	Artist	Dance	Speed MPM Length	F-D	M-S	First Dance
Samba Pa' Ti	Santana	Samba/Bossa Nova	Slow 41 4:45	✓	✓	

TABLE 3E.SLOW DANCE

First Dance and Parent Child Songs

(Note: F-D refers to Father-Daughter Dance and M-S refers to Mother-Son Dance.)

Song	Artist	Dance	Speed MPM Length	F -D	M-S	First Dance
(Every-thing I Do) I Do It For You	Bryan Adams	Nightclub Two Step or Slow Dance	Ideal 32 6:34			✓
A Love That Will Last	Renee Olstead	Slow Dance	Slow 20 3:31			✓
A Whole New World	Peabo Bryson	Rumba or Slow Dance	Slow 27 4:10			✓
Close to You	The Carpenters	Slow Dance	Ideal 22 3:42	✓	✓	✓
Dance With Me	Anthony Carter	Slow Dance	Ideal 27 3:29			✓
Endless Love	Diana Ross & Lionel Ritchie	Slow Dance	Ideal 24 4:29			✓
For Once in My Life	Michael Bublé	Slow Dance	Ideal 24 2:33			✓

Song	Artist	Dance	Speed MPM Length	F-D	M-S	First Dance
For Once In My Life	Stevie Wonder	Foxtrot, Swing, or Slow Dance	Slow or Ideal 27 2:50			✓
Grow Old With You	Adam Sandler	Slow Dance	Ideal 26 1:55			✓
I Knew I Loved You	Savage Garden	Nightclub Two Step or Slow Dance	Ideal 43 4:11			✓
In Your Eyes	Peter Gabriel	Slow Dance	Slow 22 5:27			✓
Let Your Love Flow	The Bellamy Brothers	West Coast Swing or Slow Dance	Ideal 27 3:17	✓	✓	✓
Longer	Dan Fogelberg	Slow Dance	Slow 19 3:13			✓
Lovin' In My Baby's Eyes	Taj Mahal	Slow Dance	Ideal 21 2:39			✓
Making Memories Of Us	Keith Urban	Slow Dance	Ideal 26 4:11			✓

Song	Artist	Dance	Speed MPM Length	F -D	M-S	First Dance
My Girl	The Temptations	Slow Dance	Slow 26 2:58			✓
Sea of Love	The Honey-drippers	Slow Dance	Slow 20 3:03			✓
The Look Of Love	Diana Krall	Nightclub Two Step or Slow Dance	Ideal 47 4:42			✓
The Prayer	Celine Dion and Andrea Bocelli	Slow Dance	Slow 18 4:27			✓
This I Promise You	N Sync	Nightclub Two Step or Slow Dance	Ideal 42 4:26			✓
This Will Be Our Year	The Zombies	Slow Dance	Ideal 25 2:07			✓
True Compan-ion	Marc Cohn	Rumba or Slow Dance	Ideal 28 4:06			✓
Truly Madly Deeply	Savage Garden	Nightclub Two Step or Slow Dance	Ideal 42 4:37			✓

Song	Artist	Dance	Speed MPM Length	F -D	M-S	First Dance
Unchained Melody	The Righteous Brothers	Slow Dance, Rumba or Nightclub Two Step in 6/8 timing	Ideal 33 3:36			✓
Unforget-table	Natalie Cole and Nat King Cole	Slow Dance	Ideal 21 3:30	✓	✓	✓
Valentine	Martina McBride and Jim Brickman	Slow Dance	Ideal 24 3:12			✓
When I Fall In Love	Céline Dion and Clive Griffin	Nightclub Two Step or Slow Dance	Ideal 36 4:21			✓
You & Me	Dave Matthews Band	Slow Dance	Ideal 23 5:40			✓
You Raise Me Up	Josh Groban	Slow Dance	Ideal 28 4:01	✓	✓	✓
Blessed	Elton John	Slow Dance	Ideal 25 4:22	✓	✓	

Song	Artist	Dance	Speed MPM Length	F -D	M-S	First Dance
Butterfly Kisses	Bob Carlisle	Nightclub Two Step or Slow Dance	Ideal 40 5:38	✓		
Dance With My Father	Celine Dion or Luther Vandross	Nightclub Two Step or Slow Dance	Ideal 41 4:38	✓		
Father And Daughter	Paul Simon	Slow Dance	Ideal 27 4:10	✓		
Here for You	Neil Young	Slow Dance	Ideal 27 4:29	✓	✓	
Kind and Generous	Natalie Merchant	Slow Dance	Ideal 23 4:01	✓	✓	
Memories	Elvis Presley	Slow Dance	Ideal 22 3:05		✓	
My Girl	The Temptations	Slow Dance	Ideal 26 2:58	✓		
Song for My Son (Maybe You'll Never Know)	Winsome	Slow Dance	Ideal 27 3:25		✓	

Song	Artist	Dance	Speed MPM Length	F -D	M-S	First Dance
You've Got A Friend	James Taylor	Nightclub Two Step or Slow Dance	Ideal 46 4:30	✓		

TABLE 3F.SWING

First Dance and Parent Child Songs

(Note: F-D refers to Father-Daughter Dance and M-S refers to Mother-Son Dance.)

Song	Artist	Dance	Speed MPM Length	F-D	M-S	First Dance
Ain't That Love	Ray Charles	Foxtrot, Swing, or West Coast Swing	Ideal 30 2:51			✓
For Once In My Life	Stevie Wonder	Foxtrot, Swing, or Slow Dance	Slow or Ideal 27 2:50			✓
Loves Me Like a Rock	Paul Simon	Swing	Ideal 36 3:32		✓	

TABLE 3G.TWO STEP

First Dance and Parent Child Songs
Note that Two Step (a country dance) and Nightclub Two Step (a "love song" dance) are completely different dances (see Dance Descriptions below).

(Note: F-D refers to Father-Daughter Dance and M-S refers to Mother-Son Dance.)

Song	Artist	Dance	Speed MPM Length	F-D	M-S	First Dance
Forever and Ever, Amen	Randy Travis	Two Step	Ideal 45 3:32			✓
Forever And For Always	Shania Twain	Two Step	Ideal 43 4:43			✓
Sweet Thing	Keith Urban	Two Step	Ideal 51 3:48			✓
Daddy's Hands	Holly Dunn	Two Step	Slow 38 3:29	✓		

TABLE 3H.VIENNESE WALTZ OR HESITATION WALTZ

First Dance and Parent Child Songs
(Note: F-D refers to Father-Daughter Dance and M-S refers to Mother-Son Dance.)

Song	Artist	Dance	Speed MPM Length	F -D	M-S	First Dance
Always And Forever	Heatwave	Viennese Waltz (advanced dancers) or Hesitation Waltz; Rumba in 6/8 for beginners	Ideal 51 6:14			✓
Colour My World	Chicago	Viennese Waltz (advanced dancers) or Hesitation Waltz; Rumba in 6/8 for beginners	Ideal 53 3:02			✓

TABLE 3I.WALTZ

First Dance and Parent Child Songs
(Note: F-D refers to Father-Daughter Dance and M-S refers to Mother-Son Dance.)

Song	Artist	Dance	Speed MPM Length	F -D	M-S	First Dance
Anniversary Waltz	Tony Evans And His Orchestra	Waltz	Ideal 31 2:18			✓
Between Now and Forever	Bryan White	Waltz	Fast 36 3:17			✓
Could I Have This Dance	Anne Murray	Waltz	Ideal 30 3:16			✓
Fascination	Nat King Cole	Waltz	Ideal 29 2:30			✓
Give Me Forever (I Do)	John Tesh	Waltz	Ideal 35 3:50			✓
I Will Always Return [Soundtrack Version (End Title)]	Bryan Adams	Waltz	Ideal 32 2:46			✓
Kiss From A Rose	Seal	Waltz	Fast 44 4:49			✓

Song	Artist	Dance	Speed MPM Length	F -D	M-S	First Dance
My Cup Runneth Over with Love	Ed Ames	Waltz	Ideal 33 2:44			✓
One Hand, One Heart	From the Album Forever Mine - Wedding Songs	Waltz	Ideal 34 3:03			✓
Open Arms	Journey	Waltz	Ideal 34 3:19			✓
Take It to The Limit	Eagles	Waltz	Ideal 30 4:46			✓
Tea-House Moon	Enya	Waltz	Slow 26 2:43			✓
The Lover's Waltz Duet	Jay Ungar And Molly Mason	Waltz	Fast 36 3:27	✓	✓	✓
The Sweetheart Tree	Johnny Mathis	Waltz	Slow 28 2:14			✓
Their Hearts Are Dancing	The Forester Sisters	Waltz	Ideal 33 3:43			✓

Song	Artist	Dance	Speed MPM Length	F -D	M-S	First Dance
When I Need You	Leo Sayer	Waltz	Fast 36 4:13			✓
With You I'm Born Again	Vanessa Williams and George Benson	Waltz	Slow 27 3:53			✓
You Light Up My Life	Whitney Houston	Waltz	Ideal 31 3:41			✓
You Make Me Feel Like A Natural Woman	Aretha Franklin	Waltz	Ideal 35 2:47			✓
A Song for My Son (Traditional OR Country versions)	Mikki Viereck OR Donna Lee Honeywell	Waltz	Fast OR Ideal 38 OR 33 3:05		✓	
Goodnight, Demon-slayer	Voltaire	Waltz	Fast 41 4:49	✓	✓	
Daddy's Little Girl	Al Martino	Waltz	Ideal 30 2:32	✓		
Mama	B. J. Thomas	Waltz	Ideal 32 2:59		✓	

Song	Artist	Dance	Speed MPM Length	F -D	M-S	First Dance
Sunrise, Sunset	Complete Wedding Music Resource	Waltz	Ideal 35 4:15	✓	✓	
Tea-House Moon	Enya	Waltz	Slow 26 2:43	✓	✓	
Turn Around	Perry Como	Waltz	Ideal 31 2:30	✓		
What The World Needs Now Is Love	Jackie Deshannon	Waltz	Fast 36 3:15	✓	✓	

TABLE 3J.WEST COAST SWING

First Dance and Parent Child Songs

(Note: F-D refers to Father-Daughter Dance and M-S refers to Mother-Son Dance.)

Song	Artist	Dance	Speed MPM Length	F-D	M-S	First Dance
Ain't That Love	Ray Charles	Foxtrot, Swing, or West Coast Swing	Ideal 30 2: 51			✓
Let Your Love Flow	The Bellamy Brothers	West Coast Swing or Slow Dance	Ideal 27 3:17	✓	✓	✓
Never Had Nobody Like You	M. Ward	West Coast Swing or Rumba	Ideal 30 2:26			✓

TABLE 3K.MEDLEY

First Dance and Parent Child Songs

(Note: F-D refers to Father-Daughter Dance and M-S refers to Mother-Son Dance.)

Song	Artist	Dance	Speed MPM Length	F-D	M-S	First Dance
I'm Sticking with You	The Velvet Underground	Medley	Fast 48; 18; 41 2:28			✓

Dance Descriptions

When you decide to pick a specific dance style, for your various wedding dances, it is important to consider the descriptions of those dance forms. Knowing the basics of any dance type is essential to get a rough idea of how the dance will need to be performed. Listening to the songs that have been specifically mentioned as songs most appropriate to particular dance forms will make it even clearer for you to understand how it might look or sound.

Descriptions of the most popular dance forms have been given below for your consideration. These basics about each dance type will help you understand the dance better and make an informed decision.

Foxtrot

The foxtrot is a ballroom dance, which is perhaps the most popular social dance in the world today. This American dance originated in 1913 when, vaudeville performer, Harry Fox and his partner performed a "trot" to Ragtime music (the original form of Jazz). "Fox's Trot" appealed to the social dance teachers in New York at the time, and thus the foxtrot was born.

Through the years, both the music and the dance have evolved into the smooth and sauntering dance that we see today. Foxtrot music is played by most social dance orchestras and is one of the easier dances to learn.

Foxtrot is typically danced to jazz or Big Band type music, the same type of music that you would use for swing dancing. Speed is usually the deciding factor that makes a song better for foxtrot or swing (foxtrot being slower usually), although it is fun and not too difficult to switch back and forth between foxtrot and swing in the same dance.

Foxtrot is danced in closed dance position (facing your partner and holding each other close). The most common Foxtrot rhythms are slow-slow-quick-quick or slow-quick-quick, slow-quick-quick, where "slows" are defined as 2 beats of music per step and "quicks" are defined as 1 beat of music per step.

Nightclub Two Step

One of the most practical and versatile social dance forms ever developed, nightclub two step should not be confused with country/western two step dance form.

It is designed to be used with contemporary soft rock, especially "love songs". This type of music is common just about everywhere - at weddings, nightclubs, on the radio, etc. Hence, this dance form is easy to fit into any occasion. The rhythm of the dance is very simple: 1&2, 3&4, also counted as quick-quick-slow, quick-quick-slow – or if it fits the song better, the rhythm can be reversed: slow-quick-quick, slow-quick-quick.

This romantic dance fills a gap where no other ballroom dance fits. The technique is not as rigid as the traditional ballroom dances, and the dance is easy to learn. The nightclub two step can be a very romantic dance (although, as with any dance, the romance factor can be left out when, for example, dancing with a parent).

Rumba

The rumba is characterized by the swaying of hips from side to side, in what has come to be known as "Cuban Motion." The rumba is often referred to as the "dance of love." Sultry and romantic, the music is traditionally a mixture of African and Latin rhythms.

Rumba, as we know it today, came mainly from Cuba, although there were similar dance developments, which took place in other Caribbean Islands and Latin America in general. The "rumba influence" came to the Caribbean Islands and Latin America in the 16th century when slaves were imported from Africa. There are a few different types of Rumba dances with slight variations such as Cuban Rumba, Flamenco Rumba and African Rumba.

The native rumba folk dance was essentially a pantomime of sex, danced with exaggerated hip movements. The dance was frowned upon by high society, although eventually the dance became acceptable and highly popular across all segments of society.

Rumba has morphed over time, but it maintains the spirit and soul of Latin American music and dance, including sensual hip movements, and is today one of the most popular ballroom dances. As with any dance, the sexiness factor can be turned down when dancing with someone other than your partner, for example a parent.

Samba/Bossa Nova

Samba is a lively, rhythmical dance of Brazilian origin. There are two major streams of Samba that differ considerably: the modern ballroom Samba, which is a partner dance (which is what you would dance as a wedding dance), and the traditional Samba of Brazil, which is solo folk dance (which you might see in Brazilian carnival and elsewhere).

Samba, as a partner dance, first became popular internationally in the 1920's and 30's, although it was modified from the original folk to make it suitable for partner dancing.

Samba music has a joyful, contagious rhythm, which can be found in many popular songs today. To achieve the true character of the Samba, dancers must give it a happy, flirtatious, and exuberant interpretation. Many dance steps used in the Samba today require a pelvic tilt (Samba tic) action, which can be difficult to accomplish. However, without the Samba tic, the dance loses much of its character.

The Samba is now a moderately popular ballroom dance, usually limited to experienced ballroom dancers because of its speed. However, a slow Samba is something that beginners might actually enjoy doing.

Bossa Nova has its roots in the Samba, with movements that are soft and flowing, with plenty of side steps and hip sways. It is one of the less popular forms of partner dance taught today, quite possibly because the music is so laid back and relatively uncommon. It sounds much like a slow, "lazy" Samba, and Bossa Nova's moves match the sound of the music. In fact, many Samba patterns can be danced slower and with less energy, more or less turning the steps into Bossa Nova. Conveniently, this works well as a wedding dance option.

Slow Dance

Slow dance can be extremely romantic and sensual, if done the right way. "Slow dancing" can refer to any type of partner dance, which a couple dances slowly, swaying to the music. It is often associated with a simple style of dance performed (usually awkwardly) by middle school and high school students, and also by many wedding couples, where the man typically holds his hands against the sides of the woman's hips or waist while she drapes her hands on his shoulders. Foot movement is minimal - the couple typically sways back and forth with the music, possibly moving slowly in a circle. The dance (though perhaps fun to do) is boring to watch when done this way and is not often considered to be a "real dance."

However, there is much more you can do in Slow Dancing, turning it into a "real dance", which is far more enjoyable for your guests to watch and for you to dance. With just a little instruction, you can learn to have a proper dance frame, do lead and follow, and perform real steps, including turning together, moving around the floor, turning the lady in an underarm turn, and so forth. If you choose a song that is too slow for rumba, learning a little slow dancing is your best bet.

Because slow dancing is not an officially recognized dance, you may have trouble finding an instructor to teach you this style of dance. Hence, probably getting DVDs to learn this style of dancing (see section below) is a better option. It is a very easy dance to learn and many couples do it for their First Dance, so have fun with it!

Swing

"Swing" refers to a group of dances that developed concurrently with the swing style of jazz music in the 1920s through 1940s. The best known of these dances is the Lindy Hop, a popular partner dance that originated in Harlem in the African American community and is still danced today. As the music changed between the 1920's and 1990's, the Lindy Hop, Jitterbug, Lindy, and other forms of swing evolved across the U.S. with many regional styles.

From the mid 1940's to today, ballroom dance teachers have created a syllabus of common swing steps to facilitate teaching swing, resulting in East Coast Swing, which is taught and danced throughout the country. There are also swing dance communities in many countries throughout the world, and each local swing dance community has a distinct local culture and defines "swing dance" and "appropriate" swing music in different ways.

Two Step

The country/western two-step, often called the "Texas two-step" or simply the "two-step," is a country/western dance that is usually danced to lively country music. It is a progressive dance that proceeds counterclockwise around the floor, as do all other progressive dances, although as a wedding dance with no other couples on the floor, you can dance around the floor however you like.

The two step (as we know it today) derived from the American style foxtrot (also borrows dance steps from swing), and the basic timing is quick-quick-slow-slow.

Waltz

Waltz is considered to be one of the most romantic and elegant dances of all time. Graceful turns, elegant sweeping movements and stylish poses are characteristic of waltz. The most distinguishing feature of the waltz is that the music is in groupings of 3 beats, rather than the more common groupings of 2 or 4. Waltz is counted 1-2-3 with a heavy accent on the 1. You cannot dance other dances such as foxtrot to waltz music because of this three-beat grouping.

When waltz became popular with Austrian aristocracy in the 18th century, it was scandalous. Until that time, the aristocracy danced with their partners in an open position, touching only hands. The closed position (with the partners face to face and holding each other close) of the waltz caused an uproar, considered by many to be immoral and obscene. But times changed, and by the late 1800's the waltz was generally accepted by polite society, and eventually many more closed partner dances, such as the foxtrot and the tango, were developed.

Waltz has continued to rise in popularity, and is commonly danced at weddings, anniversaries, graduations, and ballroom dances across the world.

Hesitation Waltz

The hesitation waltz is a variety of waltz that is relatively easy to learn if you can dance regular waltz. Hesitation waltz is danced to fast waltz music (the same music as the Viennese waltz), but is easier to learn than Viennese Waltz. The defining characteristic is that it incorporates many "hesitations", where you step on beat 1 and hold during beats 2 and 3 (with the other foot suspended in the air or dragging on the floor).

The hesitation may be used whenever desired - every measure (measure = one set of 1, 2, 3), every other measure, or somewhat randomly. The ways of dancing the hesitation waltz are many and varied, and there is no particular version that is more official or correct than any other.

Viennese Waltz

The Viennese Waltz is a fast waltz (about twice as fast as regular waltz), which originated in Austria with composers such as Johann Strauss writing some of the first waltzes in the early 19th century.

The Viennese waltz is danced by almost continuously turning one way, then the other. The dance looks dramatic and has been used in many Hollywood movies. It is not a beginner-level dance.

West Coast Swing

The West Coast Swing (WCS) is a gorgeous partner dance that evolved from earlier forms of swing, when Blues music became popular. It is now danced to anything from Contemporary, Country Western, R&B, Blues, Beach, Soul, Jazz, Club, Funk, and probably other types of music as well.

It is characterized by a distinctive elastic look that results from its basic extension-compression technique of partner connection, an obvious stretching, rubber band-like, in-and-out movement that creates drama and sensuality in the dance, for both the dancers and those watching.

The dance allows for both partners to improvise steps and body movements while dancing together. It is the only partner dance that allows (in fact, encourages) the woman to stylize her movements (including footwork) within the framework of the man's lead. West Coast Swing involves the entire body in the expression of subtle nuances, including body rolls, head whips, isolations, and arm and hand movements. Good dancers also incorporate "hits" in the music into the dance. In West Coast Swing, there is a definite feeling of union, merging, becoming one with the partner and the music.

West Coast Swing is a difficult, yet very rewarding, dance to master. If you don't already know West Coast Swing, it probably isn't your best choice for a wedding dance, unless you are prepared to commit a lot of time and energy to learning it. It is not a beginner-level dance.

Dance Instruction Videos

Most couples like to choose a specific dance style and invest time and effort in rehearsing their First Dance performance, before the wedding. If you want to do a specific dance but do not know the dance steps yet, you have several options.

We believe that the best, most efficient, option is to take private dance lessons so that you can focus on exactly what you need to learn. Group lessons are less expensive, but not as efficient – you won't be focusing on your specific goals, although group classes can be a lot of fun and you can get to meet new people. However, due to time, money, availability of lessons, or any number of other reasons, learning at home from videos may be a better choice for you. If that is the case, consider the following beginner-level DVDs:

- **You Can Dance – Waltz** by Vicki Regan
- **You Can Dance – Foxtrot** by Vicki Regan
- **You Can Dance – Rumba** by Vicki Regan
- **Wedding Dance DVD - easy classic slow dance** by Christel Trutmann and Kurt Lichtmann
- **Slow Dancing for Beginners Volume 1** by Shawn Trautman
- **Slow Dancing for Beginners Volume 2** by Shawn Trautman
- **Slow and Romantic Dance Sampler (Slow Dance, Rumba, Waltz, and Nightclub Two-Step)**by Shawn Trautman
- **Two Step for Beginners Volume 1** by Shawn Trautman

All of these DVDs can be found on http://www.amazon.com

Two Step (a country dance) and Nightclub Two Step (a "love song" dance) are completely different dances, as noted in the dance descriptions in the previous section.

Printed in Great Britain
by Amazon.co.uk, Ltd.,
Marston Gate.